"Whatever . . . love is love. As simple as it sounds, it is hard to practice and proclaim. By flipping labels to embrace only the 'ones we give ourselves,' Maria reminds us that how we love defines us more than whom we love."

—**Geralyn White Dreyfous**, cofounder of the Utah Film Center

"Maria has taken the courageous step of sharing her amazing story with the world, and by doing so, she benefits thousands of LGBT people and their families, and asks them to live truthfully. *Whatever . . . Love Is Love* speaks to the very heart of our fight for equality for all Americans."

—**Anastasia Khoo**, director of marketing for the Human Rights Campaign

"Maria invites us to *be* love. Separation leads to war, and connection leads to peace. She has revealed through *Whatever . . . Love Is Love* the path to peace both inside and out."

—**Jodie Evans**, cofounder of CODEPINK: Women for Peace

"In a world preoccupied with parsing the tiniest differences into yet another label, Maria Bello's bracing, heartfelt, and humane book reminds us that it's not form that matters, it's content. Love comes in so many sizes and shapes, and it's always beautiful. *Whatever . . . Love Is Love* reclaims the word 'whatever' and changes it from a nonchalant shrug into a posture at once defiant and embracing."

—**Michael Kimmel**, distinguished professor of sociology and gender studies, Stony Brook University, and author of *Guyland*

"Maria has the courage to bravely confront and challenge the labels we've been given. *Whatever . . . Love Is Love* is a provocative and thought-provoking book that makes us question the labels we struggle with and gives us hope to discover our true purpose and God-given identity."

—**DeVon Franklin**, president/CEO of Franklin Entertainment, author, and motivational speaker

Whatever . . .

Love Is Love

～

Whatever . . .

Love Is Love

Questioning the Labels We Give Ourselves

MARIA BELLO

DEY ST.
AN IMPRINT OF
WILLIAM MORROW *PUBLISHERS*

DEY ST.

Names have been omitted and certain identifying characteristics of some of the individuals featured throughout this book have been changed to protect their privacy.

FIRST EDITION

Designed by Paula Russell Szafranski

Library of Congress Cataloging-in-Publication Data has been applied for.

ISBN 978-0-06-235183-8

15 16 17 18 19   DIX/RRD   10 9 8 7 6 5 4 3 2 1

For Jackson—

I will always love you more. . . .

CONTENTS

Whatever . . .

Love Is Love

PROLOGUE

The first thing I did after I fell to the floor on my knees in agony was reach for the black rosary beads that Father Ray had given me, just before he died. In between the retches and the stabbing pains in my chest, I said the Hail Mary, something I had not done in many years.

I said the prayer over and over again. The pain would stop every three minutes, and Clare would lift me back into bed and tell me to breathe. At one point I bolted straight upright, like Linda Blair in *The Exorcist*. I clutched my beads, screaming, "Something inside of me is killing me! Something is trying to come out of me! Something needs to come out of me!!"

After months of emergency room visits, tests and an operation, we did find there was something trying to come out of me; it was a previously undiagnosed parasite I had picked up from my many years in Haiti. This parasite had, in fact, been eating me alive. And while recovering in bed for the next three months, I realized there was something else eating me alive, something that also needed to come out. It was much more powerful than the parasite.

It was my story.

In the summer of 2013, while I struggled in the hospital, I realized that waiting to do something isn't always an option. In a moment, everything could end, and my stories would be lost—stories of love, partnerships, miracles, and madness that filled the hundreds of notebooks beneath my bed. During my months of recovery, I read through each one of my trusted journals, collections of my thoughts since I was a teenager.

I started with one of my favorite journals—an old, beat-up green notebook plastered with hearts. At first, I thought reading it was going to be a classic trip down memory lane. You know, stories of teenage heartbreak, details of crazy antics, and confessions of my hopes and dreams. But something unexpected happened as I read. I began to ask myself questions. And once I started asking those questions I couldn't stop. Instead of just recovering from my illness, I found myself in the process of *un*covering who I was and who I had become.

Was I a partner?

Was I Catholic?

Was I damaged?

Were the words that I was reading the essence of who I was then, and were they still defining me now?

Who was the main character in the book of my life?

Was it the 13-year-old girl who first decided to write in her notebook covered with hearts? Was it the 19-year-old young woman whose only friend in college was an Augustinian priest? (Thank you again for those rosary beads, Father Ray.)

Was it the 20-something blonde in a ponytail marching around NYC in her army boots, pissed off at her past and anxious about her future?

Was it the 30-something woman who sounded like a teenager, thinking that every man she met would turn into Prince Charming?

Was it the woman who gave birth to an amazing kid and yet continually questioned if she was a good enough mom?

I started to see a common thread in all of the characters I had played throughout the years: a woman who was both ashamed and proud of her own truth. But, was I brave enough to let her speak?

Nope. Not exactly. Not the whole truth.

IT'S A GOOD THING MY THEN 12-YEAR-OLD SON, JACKSON, KNEW how to ask questions. Not long after my recovery, he asked me a question that would change my life forever.

My parents were visiting from Philly. Jack had willingly given up his room, adorned with a life-sized mural of a soccer player on the wall, so that his grandparents could be more comfortable. He slept in my room at the foot of the bed on a blow-up mattress at our house in Venice, CA. Surrounded by their suitcases, my dad's snoring apparatus, and my mom's prayer books, my parents dreamed away as Jack prepared to confront me one night as we were getting ready for bed.

Out of the blue, he asked me if I was currently romantically involved with anyone.

In all of 30 seconds, I flashed back across the thousands of pages in my journals. What could I tell him? Could I tell him about who I was when I was 13 years old? Or about the kind of adult I was at 32? At 47? Could I tell him the truth? The truth of how I had become the mother, lover, and woman that I am today? Could I own every bit of myself and make him understand that I will constantly evolve and change, just like he will?

I started with what he really wanted to know about—the present. His simple response when I told him I was involved with the woman who was like a godmother to him was, "Whatever, Mom . . . love is love."

JACKSON WOKE ME UP, LITERALLY AND METAPHORICALLY, WITH his statement. Our conversation opened up a door that not only led me to be brave enough to admit my truth to him, but also to proclaim it to others in a very public way.

"Whatever, love is love" was the basis of my *New York Times* article "Coming Out as a Modern Family," which was published in the Modern Love column around Thanksgiving 2013. In the article, I raised questions about the meaning of partnership, modern family, and the labels we all carry.

At the time, I had no idea how many modern families and unconventional partnerships were out there. And I didn't realize how many people did not have labels to describe themselves or the structure of their lives. So the phrase "being a whatever" came to describe them. According to the *Concise Oxford English Dictionary*, *whatever* is a pronoun "used to emphasize a lack of restriction in referring to anything." And because I am not interested in restricting myself or anyone else with a particular label, I decided that I am a "whatever," too.

Apparently I wasn't the only whatever out there. Within a day of publication, we received 273,000 Facebook posts. It was amazing that my questioning had resonated with so many people. Because of the response to my column, the *New York Times* asked me to write a second piece about why I had decided to write that first article, and to share more of my ideas.

As I read through all the blog posts, tweets, e-mails, letters, and media responses, I learned that many people in our world today are having different experiences of partnership and aren't sure how to label these different kinds of love.

Echoing the thoughts of many, one person wrote, "I've been feeling 'whatever' and I didn't know what to call it. I'm a whatever too." Another said, "Being a divorced mom I sometimes don't know where my life fits, and your story brought to light that everything doesn't always have to be black and white. There can be ex-husbands who are still partners in our and our children's lives, friends who could be lovers—whatever it is."

I was immersed in stories that were so different from mine, but also very similar. It seems that many of us have the same ideas and questions about partnerships, about family, race, religion, values, etc. I realized that there was a new conversation to be had about the labels society gives us and the labels we give ourselves.

Traditional labels just don't seem to fit anymore. These labels are limiting the possibility for people to question more and become who they are meant to be. By asking questions and challenging our own beliefs, I feel we can update all of our outdated labels and realize that labels need to evolve just like people do.

Thinking about being a whatever opened up a whole new world of intriguing questions for me. My romantic partner is fourth-generation African, so why can't she call herself an African American? My cousin Marty has dark skin but is Italian, so does she call herself African Italian? Can a gay couple consider themselves Catholic even though they are excluded from the church? Is a man who is married to a woman but kissed a boy when he was 12 considered bisexual? Are all those historical heroes of mine who also had extramarital affairs bad guys?

This book is about questions, rather than answers. Ever notice how the person who claims to have all the answers is usually a cult leader, a dictator, or just a really pushy salesperson? I am not any of those, nor am I a doctor, scientist, or therapist—even though I have actually played them on TV and in movies. What I do know is that if we keep asking really good questions about all these labels in our world, we may just come up with really good answers on how to change them. I hope that this book, and the questions posed in it, will inspire all of you to push away those labels that have been weighing you down, and force you to revel in your own experience and embrace love, family, and partnership in all possible forms.

1

AM I A PARTNER?

Who is your partner? Please take a minute to think about this question, and your most likely answer.

Looking at the people rallying around me when I was sick, I often asked myself who my partner was. To most, a partner can only be the person you are in a committed relationship with, or a business associate. Not for me. And not for my 12-year-old son, who so succinctly challenged that idea.

Two years ago, Jackson asked me if there was something I wasn't telling him. I replied, "There are a lot of things I don't tell you."

"Like what?" he asked.

"Adult stuff."

He persisted. "What kind of adult stuff?"

This was the moment I had been anticipating, even dreading for months.

"Like romantic stuff," I said, fumbling for words.

"What kind of romantic stuff?"

"Well," I said. "Like how sometimes you can be friends with someone, and then it turns romantic. Or you can be romantic, and then go back to being friends. Like with Dad and me. Or romantic like Bryn and I were, and then we became friends."

"So, are you romantic with anyone right now?" Jackson asked.

I took a deep breath, knowing that my answer, and his response, would have an impact on our lives for a very long time.

Jackson was right. There was something I hadn't told him. I was newly romantically involved, and he didn't know about the relationship yet.

I had become involved with a woman who was my best friend, and, as it happens, the person who is like a godmother to my son.

I had rarely spoken to Jack about my romantic life. That part of me I kept secret from my son. I had never introduced him to the people I had fallen in love with, or was obsessed with. It was a risk I didn't want to take. I wanted to protect him from getting attached to someone that I would probably not end up staying with.

But Clare had been with us almost daily for the last two years and I suppose he had felt our connection. She became a key part of our family in a very short time. After a week of her staying with us in LA, Jackson asked if she would be his godmother. It was no wonder that he was asking me this question now.

How and when should I tell him? When I explained the situation to my therapist, she smiled and said, "Your son may say a lot of things about you when he's older, but he will never say his mother was boring."

Her advice was to wait until my son asked. And now here he was, asking.

About a year before this conversation, I was sitting in my garden in California, looking through photos and the old journals I have kept since childhood. From the green tattered notebook with hearts drawn on the cover, to the one I started in Haiti in January 2010 after the earthquake, these journals told many stories. Yet they all seemed woven together by a similar theme.

I read about the handful of men and the one woman I had been in romantic relationships with, passages rife with pain and angst. It seemed whenever I was physically attracted to someone, I would rush to put them in the box of being my "soul mate," and then be crushed when things didn't turn out as I had hoped.

I read about the two men I fell for while working on films. I was certain each was "the one," a belief fueled by sexual attraction that told me I was in love. Only once the filming ended, so did the relationships. I read about the man who asked me to marry him over the phone, before we had even kissed. Three months later we were in his kitchen throwing steaks at each other's heads in anger.

As I continued to look through my writing and photos, I came across a black-and-white print of a photo of my best friend and me, taken on the previous New Year's Eve. We looked so happy and I couldn't help but smile. I remembered how we had met two years before; she was sitting in a bar wearing a fedora and speaking in her Zimbabwean accent.

We had an immediate connection but neither of us thought of it as romantic or sexual. She was one of the most beautiful, charming, brilliant, and funny people I had ever met, but it didn't occur to me, until that soul-searching moment in my garden, that we could choose to love each other romantically.

What had I been waiting for all of these years? My friend is the person I like being with the most, the one with whom I am most myself.

The next time I saw her, in New York, I shared my confusing feelings. We began the long, painful, wonderful process of trying to figure out what our relationship was supposed to be.

First, I wondered how the relationship would affect my son. He trusted Clare. He loved her, even. Second, I worried how the relationship might affect my career. I have never defined myself by who I slept with, but I know others have and would. Such is the nature of Hollywood, in some pockets anyway.

It's hard for me even to define the term *partner* in my life, but others would try.

For five years I considered the closest thing I had to a partner to be a dear friend who just happened to be in his seventies. He was a former producer and studio head named John Calley, and I spoke to him daily until he died. We both loved books and, being seekers in life, always worked to understand ourselves and the world more. He was the one who picked me up each time I had a breakdown about another failed romance. Because we were platonic, did that make him any less of a partner to me?

I have never understood the distinction of a "primary" partner. Does that imply we have secondary and tertiary partners, too? To me, a partner is someone you rely on in your life—for help, companionship, mutual respect, and support. Can my primary partner be my sister or child or best friend, or does it have to be someone I am having sex with? I have two friends who are sisters, have lived together for 15 years, and raised a daughter together. Are they not partners? And many married couples I know haven't had sex for years. And yet, everyone thinks of them as partners.

As Clare and I grew closer, my desire for her grew stronger, and hers for me. Eventually, I decided to share the truth of our relationship with my large, "traditional" Italian-Polish Philadelphia family.

My father's response came between puffs of his cigar while we sat on the roof of a casino in Atlantic City. "She's a good girl, good for you," he said. My mother and siblings echoed his sentiments. Maybe they weren't so traditional after all?

My feelings about attachment and partnership have always been unconventional. Jack's father, Dan, will always be my partner because we share Jack. Just because our relationship is non-sexual doesn't make him any less of a partner to me. We share the same core values, including putting our son first.

At one point during my illness that summer, I thought I might not survive. But the people who were at my bedside every day at the hospital were all my life partners: my mother, Jackson, Dan, my brother Chris, and Clare.

Clare rarely left my side and called every doctor she knew to help figure out what was wrong with me. It was Dan who brought our son to see me every day, and kept him feeling safe during such a scary situation.

It was Chris's arms I fell into when I couldn't get up. It was my mother who stroked my head for hours at a time. And it was Jackson who walked me through the halls with my IV and made me breathe.

So back to Jackson's question. Was I romantic with anyone right now?

I exhaled and finally said it: "Clare."

He looked at me for what seemed like an eternity. Then, he broke into a huge, warm smile. "Mom, whether you are lesbian, gay, bi, or transgender, shout it out to the world. Whatever, love is love," he said, with wisdom beyond his years.

I loved him so much for saying those words. "But, Jack, I'm a little scared," I said. "When I was younger, people judged you if you were in a romantic relationship with a person of the same sex, and some still do. So I'm not sure how to deal with this. But we'll figure it out together."

And we have figured it out together: Jack, Clare, Dan, and I. It's a rare weekend when we aren't all piled in the same car, driving to one of Jack's soccer tournaments. Dan makes fun of Clare for getting lost and she makes sure he always has the umbrellas, sunscreen, water, snacks, and whatever else we might need in case of a nuclear disaster.

Mostly, the four of us laugh a lot. Jackson has gotten us hooked on *Modern Family*, and in each episode he tries to figure out if Dan is Phil or Jay and if Clare is Gloria or Mitchell. (He has no doubt about which character I am: Claire.)

A woman came to my trailer on a movie set a few days after my first article appeared and thanked me for my story. She said that her ex of 10 years ago lived in her guesthouse and that her best friend lived in the room next to her, and that they all helped to raise her children.

She asked me how she could explain that to people. What could she say when strangers ask "Are you in a relationship?" or "Do you have a partner?" That she is not having sex with anyone but that she does, in fact, have partners and a family?

Since she had no label to define her or her family, I said to her, "I guess you're a whatever. And your family is a whatever, too, just like mine." We shared a classic aha moment. As soon as the words came out of my mouth, she and I found ourselves beaming with pride, in tears about our amazing families.

I realized that this was a conversation that needed to be shared. I wanted my 12-year-old son to be proud of his family and not think that our story was something to be ashamed of or was so unusual. I wanted anyone who read the articles I wrote, and lived in a situation that was not traditional, to know they weren't alone.

The label of "partner" as only your sexual partner is outdated. An updated label of partner might be anyone who is significant to you in some fundamental way. The definition of the family is changing, too, and I hope it's working to bring people together with a new respect for different kinds of relationships.

So I would like to consider myself a whatever, as Jackson said.

Whomever I love, however I love them, whether they sleep in my bed or not, or whether I do homework with them or share a child with them, "love is love." And I love our modern family. They are the air that keeps me in flight, and I would be lost without them. Maybe, in the end, a modern family is just a more honest family.

So rethink that first question for a minute. Who is *your* partner?

2

AM I A CATHOLIC?

Do you consider yourself religious? Or maybe not religious but spiritual? What do these terms actually mean to you?

When I was 18 and in my freshman year at Villanova University, I met Father Ray Jackson, a 62-year-old Augustinian priest who taught a class I was taking called "An Introduction to Peace and Justice Education."

He was a former marine, six foot two, with bright blue eyes and a wicked smile. Not only did he give me my precious black rosary beads, he also introduced me to books that radically shifted the way I perceived myself and the world.

Father Ray was my "partner" all through my years at Villanova University.

He was the person I had lunch with every day in the school cafeteria, where my grandmother worked as a salad bar lady. He was the one I talked to every day about my pain, my love life, and my fears. He held me when it looked like my mother might die from non-Hodgkin's lymphoma. And he let me scream with rage when my dad went to rehab once again. He was the one I laughed with. He was the one I felt most comfortable with during those college years when I began questioning everyone and everything.

In his class he asked us to write about our heroes. While the other kids wrote about Lee Iacocca and Madonna, I wrote about Mother Teresa, Dorothy Day, Edna St. Vincent Millay, and Jesus Christ. You'd think the erotic themes of Millay would be off-limits to a guy dressed in black robes with a silver crucifix hanging around his neck, but not Father Ray. I got an A on that paper. (I'll never know if it was Millay or Jesus who swayed him.)

Although I had been raised Catholic, I never quite believed in the full Church doctrine. That would've been impossible given that I believed then and now that women also have a calling to the priesthood; that sex before marriage is actually a wise thing to do; that people should get divorced if they need to; and that women and men should be able to marry members of their own gender if they want to. And I didn't lend credence to the greatest divide of all . . . that if you weren't baptized, like my dear Jewish aunt and uncle, you would automatically go to hell. The parables and concepts contained in the teachings of Jesus Christ, about loving your neighbor as yourself, were the things I knew in my heart to be true.

Some of these ideas Father Ray agreed with and some he did not. He didn't believe in abortion unless it was to save the life of the woman, or in case of a child conceived by rape. I, on the other hand, marched in every pro-choice rally in the Philadelphia area. Yet our differences didn't deter him from being my friend. He never judged me or tried to convert me to his point of view. Father Ray was focused on caring for the poor, feeding the hungry, and making the world a better place. I think he would have liked our new pope very much.

However, not every priest I've met in my life was like Father Ray.

In my sophomore year of high school, the priest who was the head of our school met with us in the chapel every week to discuss "Christian values." In one of the more memorable sessions, he handed all the girls yellow sheets of paper containing some provocative questions and answers:

"Have you ever thought about sex? Then you have sinned."

"Have you ever had sex? Then you have sinned."

"Have you ever let a man feel your breast? Then you have sinned."

By the time I finally got to one that said, "Have you ever masturbated? Then you have sinned," I was really upset. I raised my hand, stood up, and said, "Father, my mother is a nurse and she told us that masturbation is a normal part of sexual development." I guess the sin of speaking up might have been worse than masturbation. He turned beet red and kicked me out of the chapel. My revenge? I didn't even feel guilty.

That story is why meeting Father Ray was such a revelation. He showed me that I could be Catholic *and* have my own point of view. Early on in his service as a priest, he raised the idea of how he believed women should be able to be members of the clergy, and was immediately "exiled" to a poor parish downtown. The revolutionary bad-boy Catholics and acolytes were his heroes. I wonder how we looked, sitting in the cafeteria together, a balding gray-haired man and an 18-year-old woman with long blond hair and black army boots. I wonder if anyone at school thought we were having an affair. We never talked about sex. I had only fooled around with one guy in my life up to that point, so it wasn't an important topic to me or him, given that he was pretty much sleeping with God.

Father Ray wore a white collar (sometimes) and said mass. In my eyes, those were the only things that made him a priest in the traditional sense. He was funny and compassionate and could see the good in everyone. Long before I went to Villanova, Father Ray had become close to my mother's father, PopPop Urban. Pop-

Pop was the sacristan of the church on the campus. For those not familiar with the term, the sacristan is the safekeeper of many sacred things within the church, especially the vessel that holds the "blood of Christ" (a.k.a. the holy wine) used at communion. This was the ideal job for PopPop, who couldn't resist a good draft beer, cheap whiskey, or free wine. But Father Ray loved PopPop for his good nature and sense of joy. Over beers at a local pub near Villanova while celebrating my graduation, Father Ray revealed that "After your PopPop left, our wine bills were cut in half!" Father Ray accepted my grandfather just as he was, despite his fondness for "the drink."

Mostly, Father Ray was my friend. He made me feel responsible for every minute of the life I led. He also helped me to feel not so lonely anymore. Because I grew up near the university, my friends from high school were still nearby so I never really connected with anyone at school. My friends—Kelly, Katie, Denise, and Carolyn—were and still are some of the funniest, wisest people I know. I was questing and questioning at the time for something "bigger" in life that I wasn't finding in my peers at the university. Father Ray seemed to have so many answers. And when he didn't have an answer, he always knew the right question to ask to get to the answer.

The summer after freshman year, Father Ray asked me to do research on a book he was writing called *Dignity and Solidarity.*

My first thought was "Why me? I'm a big-time sinner! Great people might be my heroes, but I have zero in common with them." But I didn't say any of that. Instead, I agreed. I was just in awe that a grown man would actually like me and trust me enough to help him with something so important. Father Ray brought me to the third floor of the massive library at Villanova, and opened a kind of secret door behind the last row of bookshelves.

Inside was an entire room filled with books and a whole new world. Over that summer, I was introduced to the words of beautiful writers and revolutionary thinkers. For eight hours a day I sat paging through book after book on philosophy, spirituality, theology, and the random, great novel. There was *Man's Search for Meaning*, Viktor Frankl's seminal book about the Holocaust. There was Elaine Pagels's *The Gnostic Gospels;* Rainer Maria Rilke's *Letters to a Young Poet;* Simone de Beauvoir's *The Second Sex;* and works by Susan Sontag, Hermann Hesse, St. Augustine, Ernest Hemingway, Virginia Woolf, Sylvia Plath, Elie Wiesel, and countless others who had changed the world. I was supposed to find quotes and examples from these great books to back up Father Ray's theories.

I can't believe he paid me for this. I think it was something like $12 an hour, which was an extraordinary sum for me at the time. I felt like I was ripping him off, because some days I didn't do a thing but read Kate Millett's *The Basement*.

Father Ray was convinced that educating students on ideas of peace and justice would lead to a more peaceful world. He wrote that his mission was "to equip the student with the knowledge and sensitivity to live a life worthy of the highest aspirations of human kind." That's exactly what he did for me. He inspired me to learn more about how I could live a worthy life. I liked his ideas about teaching peace and justice through understanding other cultures and religions.

Because of my work with Father Ray, I began reading more about man's inhumanity to man, and the oppression of women. I couldn't believe that women were still only making 73 cents to the dollar a man was making for the same job. I was enraged that one out of three women would be raped or abused in her lifetime. I was appalled that people really believed they had the right to tell me what to do with my body. So that next summer I started interning at the Women's Law Project in Philadelphia. I firmly decided that I would pursue a career in law. I would be a women's rights attorney after graduating.

Then, as happens in most romantic comedies, a cute guy comes along and changes the course of a girl's life. In my case his name was Drew. He was in an acting class and told me I should try it as an elective.

Back then I had no idea you could become an actor. I thought you had to be born and raised in Hollywood, know how to sing and dance, and just naturally be glamorous. I was just another pretty face from the wrong side of the tracks outside of the Main Line of Philadelphia. My father was a disabled construction worker and my mom was a nurse.

But I took that acting class, and in the first session I did a monologue based on a Bob Dylan song. For the life of me, I can't remember the name of the song. I dressed up like a homeless person with old newspapers and a bottle of fake booze and waxed on. I felt like I *was* that character—disenfranchised and alone. Immediately, I knew that acting was my calling.

When I went to Father Ray with this newfound revelation I burst into tears. "Father!" I said in between sobs. "I don't know what to do. I thought I was supposed to be of service to the world and help people. Now I want to act and it seems like such a selfish profession." He just smiled and said, "Maria, you serve best by doing the thing you love most."

Father Ray had just given me the best advice of my life. He set me free. Soon after, I headed to New York to follow my new calling. I had $300 and two trash bags filled with clothes. Now, so many years later, I know I don't have to live in a mud hut bandaging children to be of service. There are millions of ways to be of service to the world, and to show what I learned from Jesus' teachings.

After I moved to New York, Father Ray came to visit a few times. I would often go to find him in the Peace and Justice Center when I went home to see my parents in Philadelphia. He also wrote me letters that I wish to this day I had saved. He was the only person, besides my boyfriend, who was invited to my 21st birthday party at my family's house. I have a photo of all of us from that night, beaming and celebrating.

Father Ray was diagnosed with a brain tumor when I was 28 years old and living in Los Angeles. I flew to Philly to see him on my way to my dream trip to Africa. When I arrived, he was lying in a tiny bed in the rectory of the church. Other priests were gathered around him. He looked tired, but smiled when I entered.

I felt honored to be there, but I was also afraid. I was feeling so much, but mostly regret at what I didn't do for him or how I failed to become the person I thought he wanted me to be. But that was all in my head. I realize now that even if I had become someone most people would judge harshly, like a prostitute or a drug addict, it wouldn't have mattered to him. Father loved me and accepted me.

By the time I had arrived, Father was so weak he couldn't even lift his hand. He asked me to feed him soup. I held the teaspoon to his lips and gently wiped the excess around his mouth.

I tried to stay positive, tell jokes, and philosophize like we always had. I asked him if he was afraid to die; he said, "No."

I asked him if he was excited to die, to have a new adventure and finally meet Jesus, Mary Magdalene, and all the other cool people he had always admired. "No," he said. And from the look in his eye I could see he was saying, "It is what it is." To see Father Ray in all of his humanity, humility, and graciousness, his uncertainty and fear of death, changed me tremendously. I thought he was a super human in many ways. I thought that since he had dedicated himself to God, he wouldn't be afraid to die. I saw that perhaps, no matter how much we believe, that journey into the unknown of death is a pretty scary thing.

I was planning on taking my first trip to Africa a few days after I visited him and asked him if I should stay at home for a while longer. I was afraid he would die and I wouldn't be there. He was adamant, though he could barely speak. "This is your dream. You have to go. I'm going to be here, don't worry."

A week into my monthlong trip, I called my folks from a gigantic satellite phone from the Serengeti. The only place I could get any reception was under a baobab tree, about a mile away from where I was staying. As soon as I heard my mom's voice, I knew. Father Ray had died the day before and I wouldn't be able to get home in time for the funeral. Instead, I started to say a prayer under the baobab tree that rapidly became a cry-ing rant.

"Why did you like me?! Why did I get so lucky that you chose me of all people? Why did you have to die when I was twelve mil-lion miles away in the middle of nowhere?" I could hear him laughing all the way from heaven.

So am I a Catholic? Let's see. My best friend was a priest and is my son's namesake. I do believe in the principles of Christ. But I also believe in some of the words of Buddha, Muhammad, and Yahweh. I believe in spiritual beings and angels and Sufis and any belief that is based in love. If you look beneath the surface of most religions, you will find a common thread. That thread is kindness and compassion.

Every time I travel, I go into a church and pray to Mary, and then I light a candle for my loved ones, especially my mother. My mother was a "good" Catholic. She went to church every Sunday and prayed the rosary every day. She taught us about prayer and our angels and heaven. One of the most moving experiences of her faith was when I was 13 years old. Her father, my PopPop, had just died. My mother, father, grandmother, and the four of us kids sat by his hospital bed holding his hand and saying, "We love you, PopPop," while he passed. We weren't afraid. My mom always explained to us that God had a plan and that my PopPop would now be looking after us all from heaven. Even now, my siblings and I pray to PopPop when we are going through difficult times. My mother showed all of us, in her actions, the power faith has in our lives.

My father still says he is Catholic, though my brother Chris tells another story. Chris was seven years old when our father took him out fishing on a Sunday morning. As they sat quietly in his tiny boat in the Sea Isle inlet, holding their lines in the water, my brother asked if it was okay that they were missing mass. Dad replied, "Son, this is my church." Today, Chris says that being out on the open water is his church, too. The silence of waiting for a fish to bite is his prayer.

As my son's father, Dan, who was also raised Catholic, and I try to get our son into the Catholic high school that he wants to go to, I wonder if my version of Catholicism will be acceptable. To apply, we need a letter from a pastor. But we don't have a pastor. Still, we pray every evening and give thanks at the dinner table. My son believes God is within him and present, and that there are angels like my Aunt Maria and my PopPop, who look out for him. And yet, here we are, struggling to find a church and pastor to sign a letter saying we are Catholic. I worry that our untraditional family is going to weigh against Jack. And I feel that would be a travesty. Because Jack labels himself Catholic. And if going to this school would give Jack a sense of belonging and comfort, I believe he should be able to go there.

I hope Jack will be admitted without question. I hope that it counts that Jack believes in everyone's right to have their own gods and goddesses. He is open and accepting. He has Muslim, Jewish, Christian, Buddhist, and Hindu friends and mentors. He has many friends who are gay. I wonder if that would be a help or a hindrance. If Father Ray were alive and in charge of that school, he would surely understand and appreciate that my son is surrounded with love, ideas, and inspiration.

My friend Camryn considers herself "Jew-ish." She doesn't follow the strict practices of Orthodox Judaism, but sees the beauty of the religion and culture and of passing that down to her son. On the other hand, my friends Al and Paola and their families are more traditional Jews. They read from the Torah, observe Shabbat, and celebrate in Hebrew. Both families include some of the most generous, accepting, soulful people I know.

My Muslim friend, Karim, is appalled at fundamentalist terrorists who say that they are following the word of Muhammad. People don't realize, he says, that most Muslims are not terrorists or jihadists and are as outraged as non-Muslims are about those who use the name of the Prophet to promote injustice and war. Does he still call himself Muslim in today's world? Yes, because he identifies with his family's history and culture. Karim believes in a God who is just and kind, just like I do.

Catholicism is part of my heritage, my upbringing, and my experience in life. It is the framework through which I extend my relationship with God. I can appreciate all religions, and still have mine. That is the kind of understanding that Father Ray taught me, and a lesson I feel lucky to have learned. As my friend Lawrence (Doobie) Nowlan said before he passed away, "I believe in my God and yours, too."

3

AM I FORGIVING?

Do you still hold on to the pain of your past? How does that pain impact you today? Do you need to forgive those in your life who hurt you to move on?

"Dad, do you remember when you chased us through the backyard with a gun?"

My sister Lisa and I are sitting with my dad in his garage. It looks exactly as it did 40 years ago. It is two weeks before Christmas and I have come back home to see everyone. Lisa and I are on the same wooden folding chairs that my grandparents, PopPop and Gram Bello, used to have in their basement. Dad sits on his walker that flips around to make a seat. He is taking drags of his cigarette in between gulps of Macallan scotch, which he always makes sure to have when I come to town. We are half a bottle in and Lisa, who is 13 years sober, is laughing.

"Ah geez," he answers, "I was on so many pain meds at that point I don't remember a goddamn thing."

I am picturing the scene, a hot summer day more than 35 years ago. We four kids and my mother marched at gunpoint with a hunting rifle through the neighbor's yard back to the home we had just run away from.

I laugh along with Lisa, but at the same time I realize how lucky we are that we *can* laugh at this. And not only us, but my two brothers, Mom, and our huge extended family, too.

I never thought that my angry, ornery giant father, who had caused me so much pain and anxiety in my childhood, would become one of my greatest teachers.

My siblings and I all agree: we were terrified of our father all the time back then. Sometimes we talk about our old war wounds and the battles we fought. We were soldiers in arms who fought side by side for many years. Our father was our common enemy. Vietnam, Philadelphia, it was all the same to us.

These days, I try to revisit my past without digging into old wounds. I spent most of my life up until I had Jack scraping off the scabs of my childhood with my fingernails until the hole got so deep it reached my bones. Those family scars never disappear entirely, but they can heal over time until they are tiny, nearly invisible lines.

Still, once in a while, even as adults, the thin lines glow a bright red and sometimes start to itch and bleed. The good news now is that we talk . . . and even laugh about the wounds that caused them.

When we were kids, we had an unspoken pact never to talk about what went on in our home. Or maybe we were afraid even then by how damaged we all were, and believed that if we started talking about it or crying about it, we'd never be able to stop. Maybe we thought silence was the only way to survive.

On the outside, we were the *perfect* family. The Bellos were the beautiful young couple with their four well-behaved, beautiful children, attending church every Sunday. But the truth was that many nights before church we were routinely awakened by our drunken father, closely followed by our crying mother, who was trying to soothe him. Dad would scream at us, "GO DOWNSTAIRS AND CLEAN THE KITCHEN! YOU LEFT IT A MESS FOR YOUR MOTHER." Terrified, we'd all scramble down the stairs to be berated and threatened by the terrifying drill sergeant for two hours. Back to sleep at five, up at seven for church, *perfect*! We were very skilled at hiding our pain, our embarrassment, and our shame.

My father, Joseph Patrick Bello Jr., was a big, strapping Italian man, who lived, breathed, danced, loved, and worked in his body. He was crushed by a steel beam on a construction site when he was 3o. He broke his back and in one second all of his dreams blew up in smoke. He was now trapped in a body that had betrayed him. Doctors gave him painkillers like candy. He didn't know he had options, or ways to find help. Instead, he thought he could handle his pain. He just didn't have the tools. My mother would try to give him the tools over the years, to "nurse him back to health." In his heart, I think he wanted to be healthy again. Aren't we all looking for someone to bandage our wounds and tell us we're okay and love us no matter what? My father was no different. But no one could give him the self-acceptance he was looking for. Not even my mom.

My mom, Kathy, was Polish, a blue-eyed, blond-haired beauty who at 15 resembled Marilyn Monroe. Looks are where that comparison stops. Kathy was known as a saint, an angel, who we always joke was so religious that she not only went to church every day, but got on her hands and knees to clean the marble floor of the vestibule while she was there. With a toothbrush. She did it all with a smile, prayerfully and joyfully.

Enter Joe Bello. He looked like Elvis, all black slicked-back hair, wild dark eyes, and slim strong body. His nickname was "Animal." He earned the name on the football field when he reached inside the rival quarterback's face mask and accidently tore his lip off up to his nose.

He fell in love with her right away. She fell in love with the bad boy. They were perfect for each other.

My mom said that after the "animal" incident, Joe Bello came to her crying. "Poor son of a bitch," he said. "What the hell did I do? Yeah, he's Irish, but he's a good guy. Why'd I do that?" And in this vulnerable moment my dad told my mom the story of what happened when he was seven years old. After Dad snuck out to ride Cousin Rusty's horse without asking, his father beat him with a belt and then tied him to a pole in the basement for the entire night as rats scurried over his ankles. He cried out all night but no one came to save him. After that evening he never really cried again.

It wasn't just that time but many that he was beaten. He was routinely told he was "good for nothing." He had to sit on my grandfather's right side at dinner so he could backhand him if a pea fell out of his mouth. In one night on the football field, all that rage just flew out toward the Irish kid. My mom saw then that he had a lot to be angry for. She had so much compassion for my dad. She saw the truth of his heart from the start and no matter how he acted, she would always love him.

But after the accident, things changed. My dad, coming from

old-fashioned Italian immigrants who had all worked construction, was especially ashamed of his inability to provide. Now my mom had to take care of him, pay off the house, pay all of our bills, and take care of the kids. He could do nothing, and he was furious about it. There were years of operations that only left him more scarred and in more pain. There were also the psychological effects. Back then he wasn't "disabled," as we say now, but a "cripple."

He was given painkillers to dull the pain. He drank to dull the pain. He sat in his orange-and-red Barcalounger for years cursing the guys who had taken his life from him. He also cursed and abused my mother, us kids, and even our dogs. He would scream and yell, throw things, and chase us through the backyard with a gun when we ran away.

He hit bottom when we discovered my mother had non-Hodgkin's lymphoma 30 years ago. She was given five months to live. My dad went out of his mind. That summer, my family was running a pizzeria down at the Jersey Shore while my mother was in Philly getting chemo. Dad spent every day raging back and forth from the pizzeria to our one-bedroom apartment next door. After nights spent drinking, he would come to the restaurant and scream. The raging stopped when he knocked me down in anger for closing up five minutes too early. My older brother threw him out of the window. We all had had enough. That was the last time my father ever laid a hand on any of us.

My father and I have healed a lot over the years. It is an ongoing process. I could always see his light, though it was painful at times. I saw how much he hated himself and how his father had passed that self-hatred down to him. I saw the possibility that I could be that way, too, if I didn't face my own demons.

After having gone through years of my own therapy and developing a deeper understanding of myself and my dad, I'm not terrified of him anymore. Now I am compassionate, painfully curious, and heartbroken for him. How must he have felt every time he had to ask one of us little kids to tie his shoe? He was in too much pain to perform even simple acts himself. Even my child self knew I was crossing some sort of dangerous territory as I dropped to my knees day after day to tie the "protector's" shoe. A man who could once lift an entire building now could not tie his shoe. I can only imagine the shame.

Now, as an adult, I can focus on the beautiful things my dad did and the sacrifices he made for us. He got up every Saturday and Sunday at 5 A.M. to drive my sister and me to our jobs at the local bakery, and my brothers to their jobs picking up nails on construction sites. He drove even though he could barely sit up straight. He taught us the value of hard work and how to become self-reliant. He made sure every one of his kids went to college and saw Disney World before we left home for good.

And now, three decades later, I am sitting in the garage with him and my sister just talking, remembering those painful and joyous moments of our childhood. I am humbled by his courage. He quit the drugs and heavy drinking. When I was in my 20s he was finally diagnosed with bipolar disorder. He started medication and has been much saner since. In my 30s, he was wrongly diagnosed with early Alzheimer's and was given more medication that made him shake so hard he couldn't bring a spoon to his mouth. He was eventually rediagnosed with multiple sclerosis. He loses more mobility every year.

But the thing that makes me honor my father most is that he was able to own his mistakes. He has apologized to all of us for years. He cannot remember most of what happened when we were younger, but he apologizes nonetheless. It hurts him deeply to know that he hurt us. And my brothers and sister and I have accepted his apologies. We better understand his illness and the grief he was plagued by when he lost the life he had.

He is a great grandfather to Jackson and his other five grandkids. They like hanging with "Pop," whether it's going fishing with him or learning to shoot pellet guns in the backyard.

He has slowed down over the years, but still comes often to

Los Angeles to see my brother and our family. Clare dotes on him as he sits on his scooter on our patio and smokes his cigarettes. (He always quits right before he comes and then starts smoking with me immediately when he gets here.) He fixes things around the house. He repaired the antique white French bistro chairs we had that were missing slats of wood. It took him six months. He sketched the exact dimensions and took them home to his workshop so he could make exact replicas. I can see the chairs now. We didn't repaint the new wooden slats to match the old white ones. And we never will. We like them mismatched. It reminds me of my dad and his endless courage and grace to overcome the worst of what life might hand him.

I don't really know how many years it took to transform my relationship with my dad, to come to a place of peace with the things that happened in my childhood. My experience with my family reminds me of the fluidity of all relationships. If we can only allow our relationships to go through their changes and get to the bottom of our own rage, sorrow, and shame, then we have the opportunity to become stronger, and more open to love.

My brothers and sister have emerged from our childhood as extraordinary human beings. They are my partners in many ways. None of my other partners will ever know what it was to grow up in that house. We have a shared experience. Instead of that making us more distant, it makes our bond stronger. My older brother, Joey, always says, "Friends will come and go, but you'll always have family." And I am confident I will always have these three in my life.

Forgiveness is said to be the only balm for old war wounds. There are so many incredible stories of forgiveness for acts that truly seem unforgivable. I am in awe of the stories of forgiveness from heroes and heroines such as Nelson Mandela, Somaly Mam, Louis Zamperini, and many others. I've ventured into the battlefield a few times over the years and always came back with the same answer. Forgiveness is complicated. It entails a rational decision. It's something you do as an adult. A child is not rational. A child just feels. I can't tell someone to forgive. My siblings and I grew up in an atmosphere of violence and unpredictability. I can't erase that, and, believe me, I have tried over the years. It is a part of me. But, yes, I have forgiven my Pop. And I can forgive others who have harmed me. But I couldn't have done that without accepting that what had happened was part of me. For me, forgiveness as an adult is really about acceptance. Though the child within you may never forgive the wrongs, perhaps the adult self should just work on accepting them.

I have come to see my father and mother as people, not just godlike figures who controlled my life. I have acceptance for where they came from, and what they were taught, who they were, and what their values are. Knowing and accepting doesn't always take the pain of what happened to our family away, but it does help us to pull away the fear and trauma and see the good inside of each other. Maybe it even helps us to forgive *ourselves* a little more. And I know, it is far better to be a forgiver than to be bound by anger.

4

AM I A BAD GIRL?

Have you done something you're supposed to be ashamed of?

I am watching the married man I had an affair with for two and a half years kissing another woman in a movie. I heard he was actually having an affair with the actress in real life. Now I know how his wife must have felt back then.

At first, I wasn't going to turn on the movie. But that night, after being alone for many hours, I decided to turn it on. I was riveted. The man I'd been involved with hadn't even appeared yet, but I was loving the plot and the lead female character and the actor who was portraying her. She was strong, beautiful, and brilliant. Everything out of her mouth seemed true. She fully inhabited that character. And when my still-married ex-lover popped on the screen, I didn't instantly think, "They're having an affair." I thought, "He's a really bad actor."

At the time I was involved with him, he was the love of my life.

We met years ago at an industry event. When we first shook hands, I was taken with his good nature and all-American good looks. I also noticed his gold wedding band. I did not have a band but had been in a serious relationship for many years. By the time I met him, that relationship was on the rocks mostly because of my inability to commit and my continuous search for the one. At that moment I didn't even consider the man a potential, with the ring and all. It wasn't till a week in that I was overtaken with a desire akin to a tsunami. A few weeks later, we began an affair.

Within a week, my current relationship began unraveling. My heart was opening and breaking into pieces at the same time. I had lied to the man I was with, hurt him terribly, and felt shame and remorse. At the same time, I was allowing myself to completely give in to my desire for this other man. These were complicated feelings, all of them, smashed up together.

After our first 10 days together—he went back to his suburban life, and I went back to the carnage of mine—I got an e-mail from him that read:

My love.

*I can't do it. I can't leave my kids. As much as I love you,
I cannot do it. They are at a very vulnerable age. My wife
is a good woman. We've had a partnership—have for
many years. But you must know that you are the most
extraordinary woman I have ever met. You are definitely
the sexiest. If I could I would live my life with you. Yes,
we could try to continue the half-ass thing that we had
for a couple of weeks (stolen moments and all). But it is
not fair to you. You deserve to be loved fully and without
reservation. I'm sorry to savage your heart again. I truly
am. I am still in love with you and will be for the rest of
my life. Good-bye my girl.*

Yours.

Me.

I got this missive and about 200 similar ones from him over
the next two years.

Our letters were always filled with drama, breaking up and
not being able to keep away from each other. In retrospect, it was
a lot like the good old-fashioned romance novels I read as a teenager, minus the storybook ending, of course.

Here's what our "relationship" looked like for years: He would sneak away to Los Angeles or me to New York for a day or two. We would meet at my house in LA, a hotel in NYC. We would immediately find ourselves in bed. And after hours, we would make great meals together and laugh and talk and share. And then we would go back to bed. It would have been a month or a week from the last time we were together. But we couldn't help seeing each other again even though every time we said it was the last. And we had mind-blowing sex. Eye-to-eye, raw-animal, but loving sex. I had never had sex like that before. And then again, I had never been with a married man before. The secrecy made the rush that much more intense.

Afterward, we would lie side by side talking, dreaming of what our life could be together. We would go to Africa or to a fishing camp in New Zealand, where he had just shot a movie. I would wear my brown bikini and we would get lost on a beach in the middle of nowhere. We would go to Machu Picchu and Brazil. We would meet fabulous people and tango all night. Or we would just walk hand in hand in my Venice neighborhood, eat burritos at Stroh's deli, and read the *New York Times* on Sunday. Our first trip would be to Mexico. We would proclaim our love. He would tell me that I was the one and he would never leave me. And for a few days, a few weeks, we would live this dream. And just as suddenly as it started, it stopped.

I knew the relationship was finished a few weeks before it officially ended, when my friend John and I sat in a café in Venice having lunch. John liked this man and liked that I was happy with him. I remember John saying to me, "He is nice and not an asshole. But, if he wasn't great in bed, would you still be interested in him? What if he was in an accident and his dick fell off, would you still want him?"

John described him and me as bifurcated. This man wanted his family and could be entirely present with them. Yet, he would call me in the middle of his kid's football game. I too was bifurcated. I liked the pleasure of our relationship, but I was pained by the baggage. When it got to the place where we went away for a weekend but couldn't hold hands walking from store to store, it was a big wake-up call. As much as I liked the secrecy, passion, and drama, I liked living life in the open much more.

Now, sitting on my couch watching the married guy on television, I hear him calling the actress with whom he is having an affair "sweet baby" and I can't believe what I am hearing. I remember a real scene like this, years ago in my kitchen in Venice.

"How's my sweet baby?" he would say, walking into my kitchen and taking me into a big bear hug.

"I'm good today, baby. How are you?" I would ask. And I was good. I felt strong and resilient in his presence.

"Well, let's see, I've just spent the night with the love of my life, my favorite playmate, my sweet baby, I think I'm pretty good."

And now this "sweet baby" wants to vomit. This is who he is and might always be. I wonder if the other actress knows yet.

I made similar mistakes over the years, but never again with a married man. I would choose men and think that the adrenaline high I got from the push and pull wasn't just sex but was actually love. It was a hard lesson: adrenaline does not equal love. But it doesn't negate it either.

The definition of desire is to want something you do not have. In a marriage, or other committed relationships, especially after years together, each person seems to know the other inside and out. They *have* the person so it may become difficult to desire them. Some people seek sexual satisfaction outside their relationships, even though they may be totally sure that they would not leave their committed partner or family. The truth is, we have no idea what goes on in people's bedrooms or in their heads. Some people place more value on partnership than sex. But sex in secret holds appeal for many.

Many of my heroes have had sexual relationships outside of their committed relationships. But does that make them bad people, or take away the fact that they have contributed to this world in incredible ways? Many wives of men who have cheated stay with their husbands, and certain people are appalled by that. I'm not. I understand. To me, sexual desire and love are two different things. That certainly doesn't mean that people inside of long-term committed relationships don't have great sex. I know some who do. But not many, if I'm honest. Those who do often say the same thing, "It comes and goes." And maybe it does. But let's be real, for many it just goes. And then what happens? People either start to lie and look outside of their relationship, or they find a way to make it work. I was told by a therapist many years ago that I just needed to heal my "daddy issues" and then I would be able to have guilt-free sex with a man I was not in love with. She wasn't a very good therapist.

It has been written that all but two of our presidents have had affairs. I'm not sure I believe the number, but it sure makes me very curious. JFK, Martin Luther King Jr., and so many others who made the world a better place were considered adulterers. Does that make them bad people? And it seems to me that the people who point the fingers are often just as guilty, if not more so.

One of my friends has been married for close to 20 years. She has beautiful children, is funny and compassionate and sexy. So was her husband. She found out last year that this kind man was not only having affairs, but much worse. This great dad, and I won't take that away from him, was having group sex with different swingers almost every day for years. Can you imagine? My friend thought they were best friends. She said what I've heard many people say: it wasn't the infidelity that was the worst part, it was the lying and the disregard he had for her. This is an extreme circumstance, but is this man a criminal? Certainly not to his kids.

I believe that the book *Fifty Shades of Grey* became a worldwide phenomenon because people were finally given a chance to explore their fantasies in a safe way. Many authors have done the same throughout the years. If you were turned on by *Fifty Shades of Grey,* go read Miller or Nin or Hemingway or Roth or Edna St. Vincent Millay.

Most people will never admit their sexual proclivities. You usually have no idea what your partner is thinking about when having sex. Could be he/she is thinking of kittens and feet. Unless you are in someone's bed and someone's head, someone's sexuality should be no business of yours. So a call to action to all therapists, please keep trying to isolate the gene that makes all of us confused about our sexuality. But maybe we aren't sick after all. Maybe there is no "cure" and we should just accept that sexuality is more complicated and fluid than we've been led to believe. Whoever has a handle on sexuality, our unconscious, and why we are often blinded by desire please let me know.

So does my having an affair with a married man make me a bad girl? If the answer is categorically yes or no then we're all missing the point. Yes, I hurt people I loved, and I take responsibility for that. I also found a freedom in expressing my sexuality that I hadn't felt before. I began to understand that for many people, sex does not equal love and that our primal physical drive isn't necessarily bad. Sometimes, two people can just admit their connection is not sexual, but they share the same values, ideas, likes and dislikes, family and friends. And, at a certain point in life, sexuality doesn't seem all that important. I'm just at the beginning of my romantic relationship with Clare and we are still in the discovery stage. Will it be that way forever? Probably not. As much as we hate to admit it, people do not stay the same and neither will we. Relationships change constantly. I think if we are conscious enough, we can accept the change without throwing out the love. I am grateful to say that most of the people I've been in romantic relationships with remain my friends and family. And I've been on both sides. Partners of mine have had affairs. Though it was incredibly painful, I eventually and quite quickly saw the humanness in all of it.

I sometimes find the most difficult thing is to live in the gray area of life—to live in the indecision, to listen to all of the voices screaming inside of us to be heard, with no judgment. I could never figure out if I was a "good girl" or a "bad girl." Seems life would be so much simpler with clear definitions. At times I think I've figured out something only to be surprised in the next instant by who I am and what I'm capable of.

Clare and I have a collection of original black-and-white photos above our bed. They are stunning portraits of Georgia O'Keeffe, Beatrice Wood, Ernest Hemingway, Colette, Henry Miller, Edna St. Vincent Millay, Anaïs Nin, and other writers and artists that we admire. They have many things in common, including being people who brought to light, in words or pictures, our deepest feelings. They were also people who were passionate, had affairs, families, and lovers. Some were bisexual, some were just plain sexual. Some lied and some did not. But they all lived their passions and desires. They didn't assume that sex, family life, friendships all had to be the same, forever.

So let's not pretend that only bad people have affairs, or make decisions based on desire and animal passion. At least, let's throw out our inclination to point fingers and name names, and instead accept that we can never know what is in someone else's head, or how we might turn if overcome with feeling.

5

AM I PERFECT?

Is there a secret to being perfect?

"As much as I try, I cannot get him out of my head, even though I know he is bad for me," I said in angst to my dear friend John.

"Then I will move into your head immediately," he replied. "We'll have plenty of room once we move him out. He doesn't belong either in your head or in your bed. He just serves your addiction to pain. You're the most wonderful, gifted, brilliant, lovable woman . . . you'd have to travel far and wide to find someone damaged enough to not cherish and love you, but somehow you're able to find them. I think you're the one who's committed to hurting you. He's just a screen on which you project your cruelty to yourself. I love you very much and won't allow you to keep doing this to yourself. The 'mean you' doesn't deserve the wonderful you as a brain mate. When I get over there, we're going to move her out, too. It makes me feel sad when you are hurting so it's got to stop, because I won't leave you and I know you don't want to make me feel like shit. So it's got to stop. I love you more than you hurt."

I was walking down the path on the beach in Santa Monica with my friend John Calley when we he said this to me some years ago. John was a 70-year-old movie producer, an ex–studio head who loved books, napping, and me.

John and I met when he saw a movie of mine in 2003 called *The Cooler*. He found out who my manager was, and asked if he could meet with me. All I knew was that I was meeting with a producer who possibly wanted to offer me a job.

I was living in a loft in Venice at the time, and having a fantasy affair with an actor. I was filled with anxiety and angst. John and I were supposed to meet at a fancy restaurant in Santa Monica, but I was such a hermit then that I asked if he could meet me at a dumpy Mexican restaurant down the street from me instead.

As soon as I walked into the dimly lit place, I recognized him sitting at a booth. And not because I had already looked him up. I had no idea what he looked like, how old he was, or what his list of movies was. But I knew *him*—like I knew the willow tree in my backyard when I was growing up. He may have been the most familiar person I'd ever met for the first time.

We immediately started getting into the nitty-gritty. We never spoke about movies, the business, or any of the usual formalities. We talked about love and relationships and their complications, right away. He was warm and funny, and smart, but not in an overly earnest or smothering way. He got the humor of life. John understood that all of the serious things and all of the hurtful things we live through help us grow. From that day on, and for the next five years, we spoke almost every day.

John had a wonderful family, one of the first modern families I have ever witnessed. His modern family consisted of his stepchildren, an ex-wife, and her new husband, all of whom he adored. They lived in Canada so he didn't see them that much. He had many friends, his best friend being the late Mike Nichols. John was so respected in our business that he was almost revered. People speak of him as the most honest gentleman who ever worked in Hollywood. I was lucky to meet him some years before he died. By then, it was mostly just his dear friend Martha and I who spent time with John. We always shared our deepest thoughts with each other, either on the phone or in person.

I am going to share some of those conversations with you. Here's the backstory though: We originally had the conversations because I was developing a character based on him for a novel that I was writing at the time. We sat at my kitchen table in Venice for hours and days as I recorded some of our best talks. After John passed away, I went back to them, and I realized just how profound they were. I decided they needed to be shared, not as fiction, but as the real words of a man who had helped me accept all of the pieces of myself by sharing with me all of the pieces of himself.

At this point in my life, every man I met was the one. John understood completely.

"Jesus Christ," he said. "I was in 'obsession' for more than half my life."

When we talked about love versus passion, or if they were the same thing or mutually exclusive, he said, "Romantic love may be an illusion, but it is a powerful one. When you look back, you see that those guys are all the same, interchangeable really. One was not better than the other. The common denominator is you. You bring the passion to the table. It's you who drives it. Remember that."

Even when I had the loveliest live-in boyfriend, I was not satisfied. I was all about the chase. I loved the beginning of our courtship, the not-knowing phase, but once we settled into the routine of watching *Hoarders* at night and doing Jackson's homework together, the intensity wore off. I told John once that my boyfriend was a great companion. John said, "If you want a companion, why don't you just get a dog?"

John was funny, too.

I was driven, yet ashamed of my sexuality back then. He embraced and celebrated it, as he had with all the women he had been in love with in his life. And there were many. Some were real, some just fantasy. He constantly affirmed to me that there was nothing to be ashamed of by being a woman driven my passion.

"You are a highly sexualized woman, like all the women that you love and admire. You are Anaïs. By the way, did I ever tell you I made out with her in a closet in the Hamptons? She was hot for it even at sixty-five."

I wanted to be that woman, but at the same time I wanted to be with someone who loved and cherished me and who would never let me go.

"I love and cherish you."

"I know, but it's not the same thing. I don't have sex with you."

"If my goddamned dick worked we probably would be."

I visualized Anaïs Nin and how cool she was to live in her body and mind at the same time. She influenced my behavior sexually. With some men I even tried to be Anaïs, as highly charged, as reckless and sexually fearless. One day, in a manic state, I sat crying at 6 A.M. on a balcony at my rental apartment in Vancouver, drinking a scotch and talking to John on the phone. There was a man in the next room who I was working with, doing the push-pull dance. He had a girlfriend back in New York. We had had a terrible night, with me withholding so he would come forward, and my Anaïs act just wasn't working. I felt rejected. I knew he just wanted sex and what I really wanted was sex *and* love.

"But he is rejecting me, because he has a girlfriend," I said.

"Bullshit. He can't keep his hands off you. You're a lot better off than the model girlfriend who is at home, waiting for him to stop fooling around with you and give her a call. He's not a bad guy," John replied. "Just not plausible for you. You're right in that you made him up in your head. Who is he really?"

John was right; I had blown him up in my head to be someone or something much more important than he was. I thought he, like most of the other men, had the power to save me. I should have known better when I caught him jerking off to his own image on the Internet.

John and I would sit in a restaurant for hours as everyone looked at us as if we were having an illicit affair. The rich, dirty old man and the pretty movie star. We were used to it. If people only knew the truth, that he was completely impotent and that I was only attracted to young assholes. He had had his share of young asshole women over the years, so we had that in common, too.

"So this was back in the sixties, before you were born," John said. "This woman was the most beautiful woman I had ever seen. Anyway, I fell in love, or should I say, I fell in anxiety.

"When we were together, it was brilliant in the beginning. She was funny and charming and made me feel funny and charming. She said, on one of our first nights together, that we should just get married. I took it to mean that she was crazy about me, but then she wouldn't take my calls for a week. When she did call, I would run to her. She would suck me in with 'you're the only one' and all that shit, then she would drink a bottle of Jack Daniel's and fall asleep drunk. I really thought if she loved me, I would finally be someone."

When I asked John how he finally got over his obsession, he told me it took him about a year. He went to a healer, a woman he had heard about in Burbank. She was a nice-looking, middle-aged woman with blue eyes and white hair. She had him close his eyes and do a meditation for about an hour. He was bored out of his mind and all he could think about was the girl with the Jack Daniel's. And when he finally opened his eyes, the healer blew what she said was white light in his face and said, "Everything is now fine."

All he could think was, "Yeah right, asshole, how much do I owe you?"

It wasn't until he got into the elevator that he realized that he wasn't thinking about his obsession for the first time in a year. From that day on, his feelings were gone. He didn't know how it happened, because he didn't even believe in the white light; he just knew something had changed.

"When the anxiety was gone, so was my 'love' for her."

I asked him how I could find this lady. I needed her.

"Beats me," he replied. "That was thirty years ago. She's probably dead."

But he reminded me I didn't need this woman, I just needed to stop giving men my power. I wish I had listened.

Years later we were together, talking about *another* man I was involved with. I was again looking for a powerful man who would take me away from all my pain. I was humiliated that I had gone to his bed once again with his sweet cunning words, and then he left and didn't call for a week.

Once again John listened. Once again he had wise things to say.

"Humiliation means I should be ashamed of myself because I've done something wrong. Humility is to want to be something beyond what is actually possible for a human being to be. There is no value judgment in humility. You want to have a magical effect on him. I mean, you are valuable, but no God. No woman will fix him. Every time you *think* of him see a line with way too much intensity in it. A high-tension wire. You are trying to fix him and he is trying to get you to fix him. That is divine, not human. Take that intensity and point it upwards. To God."

The reason he knew all this stuff wasn't because he had read about it in books, he had lived it. One day, he explained to me how he came to do what he did, and how he decided to follow a different path. "I was head of a huge production company at the time. I have no idea why. I always hated the movie business, but I was good at it. But one day after too many years of the bullshit, I woke up and realized that I was so unhappy. So, I decided to go off to an island by myself and figure out what *would* make me happy."

"And you discovered that you like reading and sleeping the best, right?" I asked, because he had told me that these were his favorite activities many, many times.

He laughed. "That's right. But it took me years to figure that out. It took a long time, walking the beach every day, for me to have my breakthrough."

"What?" I wanted to know everything about this breakthrough, because I wanted one, too. Maybe if he told me the meaning of life, I thought, I would find out what would make me truly happy.

"It was just my normal morning walk. A beautiful, cold day. I don't remember what I was thinking. Probably nothing. And then I just started to cry. I looked around me and realized that I was a part of the whole universe. It was like an explosion. Like an orgasm."

"How long did it last?" I asked him, fascinated.

"About three minutes."

"Did you ever have it again?"

"Nope."

"So what was the point?"

"Hell if I know. But I did know in that moment that I had tapped into some sort of enlightenment and only wanted to continue living in it."

John always could boil things down to their sweetest essence.

Some years after we met, John was diagnosed with cancer. One of my last memories of him was his birthday before he died. Martha and I sat at his hospital bed. He hadn't spoken for days. I brought cupcakes and a CD player that looked like an old gramophone. We sat by his side and played jazz. John had started out playing in a jazz band in Greenwich Village back in the 1950s, and he loved that music. And we danced for him. He hadn't eaten for a month, but he opened his eyes. "Happy birthday!!" we screamed. He smiled and took a bite of the cupcake I fed him.

I will always recall my last conversation with John. I remember squeezing his hand. When he moved, I held it tighter.

"Here's what I know about you," I said. "You are the strongest man I've ever met. You left home at twelve to become a bus driver and ended up running a movie studio. You are definitely the funniest person I have ever met, the only one who told me that you would actually order me a pizza if I ever tried to kill myself. You always knew I loved pizza the most.

"You're the only one I can really trust with all of myself. How can I tell you what you mean to me? When you came into my life years ago, I was on the verge of another suicidal depression. A depression that drove me to the place of questioning everything I was. Was I good enough? Was the life I was living enough? Enough, enough. I was always searching for more and more ways to validate myself, to show myself how much I mattered. With you it was different. I didn't need to prove anything. You loved me for who I was and accepted me unconditionally. You never tired of my need for reassurance.

"You make me feel safe. Like no one can touch me. Like no matter what happens, there is someone who loves me. When I don't speak to you for a day I feel edgy and just not right. Whatever guys I have been through, you've never left me and never judged me. What else can I say? I love you. I don't want you to die. I couldn't handle it and wouldn't want to go on without you."

Martha called to tell me that he had died. I was numb and didn't cry until days later. I didn't go to his memorial. I didn't want to see him as some monument. I wanted to remember him in the quiet moments, the shared moments. I also wouldn't have known what to say. How could I explain to a crowd of John's friends and family how deep our relationship had been, all that

John had taught me? It was a relationship I just couldn't explain. I just wanted to remember the secret he shared with me.

"Wanna know the secret?" John whispered to me once with his eyes sparkling.

Of course I did. If anyone knew the secret to it all, it would be John.

"The secret is," he continued, "there is no secret. You are lovable just the way you are. We all walk around thinking that there is something wrong with us and that we are bad and unlovable and that everyone knows it, but the truth is there is nothing wrong with us. You are perfect. And they think so as well."

Am I perfect? In his eyes I was. Thank God I found him.

6

AM I A GOOD MOM?

Are you a good parent or the parent your child needs?

You do not have to be a parent of a child to answer this question. Your children can be your animals or nieces or nephews. It's anyone who you feel responsible for. Oprah doesn't have a child per se, but she is like a mother to many of us in the world.

Riding in our black, first edition, not-so-comfortable Prius, my then six-year-old son, Jackson, asked me an important question. Right after I just gave a guy who cut me off the finger and yelled out the window, "Fuck you, you fucking asshole!"

"Why do you curse like that and why did you yell at that man?" my son asked me. I was a little ashamed of my behavior and went silent. He continued, "And why do you smoke and be in movies? You're not like other moms." Jackson was angry and defensive when he spoke in his six-year-old way. While trying to come up with a reply that would make me sound like a good mom, a thought leapt into my head.

"OMG. This kid just nailed me. He called me out on my biggest issue—*not* being the perfect mommy." And when he persisted with more questions, like "Why don't you dress like the other moms at soccer?" I knew the answer. I am not a perfect mom. I have failed my son in many ways. But I didn't want to get into all that with my six-year-old. Did he really need to find out about his mother's neuroses so soon?

Within seconds I blurted out the only thing I could think of: "Jackson, I'm not like other mommies. I'm a different *kind* of mommy." He looked at me, and without missing a beat said, "Yeah, I get it." Then he went back to playing his game with a little smile on his face.

Goddammit! Only six years old, and the little guy had found me out. I'm not like the "other mommies." Not at all. I am not like the mommy of his friend who has just been away for a week getting breast implants requested by the rich 73-year-old with whom she's having an affair. Or the mommy of his other friend who gets stoned in the morning to face the day, then makes gluten-free buckwheat pancakes for her kids and their friends after another perfect sleepover. I'm not like the mom of his other friend who is kind, loving, and patient and does absolutely everything and anything for her kids. She doesn't go out to dinner with her girlfriends because, as her husband says, "You don't go to dinner because your kids are the most important. Those 'other' mommies are not good mommies at all."

No, I'm not like other mommies. And thank God, Jack is not like other kids. As screwed up as I sometimes think I am, Jackson just looks at me, now at 13, with a face that says, "You're crazy, Mom, but pretty cool, too." And I believe him half the time.

I recently found a letter I wrote to my dad when I was 17. It helped me understand that no matter what I did, Jackson will sometimes feel that I am not a good enough mom. This letter basically pointed out all of my father's character defects, with lines like "You use that tone with me and you've pushed all of us away." Was my dad a good enough dad then? He made mistakes, as my mother did and as do I. But he also taught me important lessons that made me the woman I am today.

I want my son to want to tell me his secrets. I want him to trust me and know I will always be there for him. And I think he does. Mostly. But when I use "that tone" like my father did with me, I wonder if he believes me when I say that I am the one who loves him most. Am I repeating the very pattern I railed against for so many years? But now I know that my dad was usually just trying to protect me and teach me a lesson when he was harsh with me. Jackson will figure that out about me someday, when he is in therapy talking about how I fucked up. Hopefully he will know deep down that I was the perfect mom for him.

My boy, Jackson Blue McDermott, is smart and funny and caring and is obsessed with soccer and FIFA Xbox games. He has always been an odd, original, wonderful duck. Jack was not your average newborn. We were told that for the first few weeks he would probably sleep on and off for 16 hours a day. Not our baby. Our baby was *awake* for 16 hours a day. He rarely slept because he was constantly interested in his surroundings, inquisitive about stuff only babies can be inquisitive about. He seemed like he wanted to *be* in the world, experience it, eat it up, and not miss a thing.

As my son grew and changed, so did I. We were both in constant periods of transition. I couldn't be a good mom to him if I treated him the same at age 12 as I did when he was 2. He was evolving and I had to evolve with him.

The definition of *transition* is "a period of changing from one state or condition to another." It can also be called a metamorphosis, or a transformation. The first time I started to understand the term was when I read a book called *Hope for the Flowers* by Trina Paulus. It was published in 1972, and still has a hippie vibe with its cover of yellow and white butterflies. I remember Sister Elizabeth, my second grade teacher, in her black habit and veil with her tiny smiling face popping out, holding up the book while she read it. We sat in our uniforms in the "reading corner" and from the first words, I was riveted.

The book is about two caterpillars: Yellow and Stripe. Though they fall in love, Stripe is obsessed with the mountain of caterpillars that thousands are climbing to reach up to the sky. They have no idea what's on top of this mountain, but everyone seems to want to climb it, so they think there must be a good reason. When Stripe decides to climb, Yellow, his girlfriend, who he has been rolling around in the fields with eating and kissing all day, is bummed. She stays behind while he climbs.

Alone and lonely now, Yellow wanders around trying to figure out what she should do next. When she sees an old caterpillar stuck in a sack in a tree and asks if she can help him get out of what looks like a trap, he says, "No, my dear, I have to do this to become a butterfly." When she hears that word, her little caterpillar ears perk up. "What is a butterfly?" she asks. The old caterpillar says, "It's what you are meant to become. It flies with beautiful wings and joins the earth with heaven. Without butterflies the earth would soon have no flowers."

"So, how does one become a butterfly?"

"You must want to fly so much that you are willing to give up being a caterpillar. This is an in-between house where the change takes place. It's a big step because you can never return to caterpillar life."

She decides to build her cocoon.

Meanwhile, Stripe is all about climbing the pile. He kind of misses Yellow, but is determined to get to the top. He makes sure not to look into the eyes of the other caterpillars. "Kill or be killed" is his driving thought. And he stomps on their heads if he has to. He becomes callous and cool and keeps climbing until he is near the top. "Yes," he thinks, "I'll show Yellow, and all of those below me, that I got to the top and beat those beneath me who were too insecure or not strong enough to make it." So he keeps climbing, at one point making it so close to the top that he can look around at all that surrounds him. He sees there are hundreds of caterpillar piles just like the one he is climbing. When Stripe finally makes it to the top, he sees the most beautiful creature flying above the pile. Yellow and kind, she looks in his eyes and he knows. It's Yellow, the hairy caterpillar he left behind.

"Oh no, I've been climbing all this time, killing people,

throwing them off of the pile to see *this*? You've got to be kidding me," he thinks. "All this way and all this work and it was just to see my girlfriend flying, looking all pretty while I'm still a hairy caterpillar?"

So in disgrace, even though he could have held on to her skinny legs and been brought down the caterpillar pile, Stripe starts down alone. Now he doesn't push others aside. He looks them in the eyes and sees the humanity in each one of them. "You are a reflection of me and I am a reflection of you. I am your brother and you are mine." He feels like an asshole remembering who he was when he was climbing. But he accepts the embarrassment and the pain he has caused others. He owns the desperation that he had felt to get what he thought would make him complete.

In the end, Stripe gets down from the pile and, soundlessly, Yellow gestures for him to build a cocoon. And he does.

Since first hearing this story in second grade, I have remembered Stripe and Yellow's journey. I wondered, even at that young age, if there was something more to life than what I saw in magazines or on television. If there was more to being happy than living in a beautiful home, having fancy cars, and wearing expensive clothes. I could be a butterfly, I thought. I don't want to be a caterpillar.

But I knew that the lesson of Yellow and Stripe was one I

wanted to teach my boy. I wanted to show him that he has his own voice and should follow his own path, not to hop on the train with assholes just because they say something is great. I want him to know that all of life is about transitions. It's about learning and becoming the best you are meant to be. But it takes a transition to do so.

When I gave birth to Jack, I *really* understood the word *transition*. In pregnancy terms it is the time between when you are screaming in agony, having contractions at seven centimeters dilated, but not allowed to push. They say it is the most painful part of labor, but also the shortest, anywhere from 15 minutes to an hour and a half. I knew mine would be very short. I had walked every day and spoke to Jack in my tummy and visualized an easy birth. "Transition is a *good* thing," my midwife said. "It means baby will be coming soon." And I believed her.

I gave birth in our home on top of Mulholland Drive in Los Angeles. I wanted the kind of "natural" birth my friends and I were so into at the time. We believed, because of our spiritual practices and study of Kundalini yoga, that the best way to give birth was with no drugs, no harsh lights, no hospitals, and no doctors with scalpels who just wanted to cut you open to get the baby out so that they could get home for dinner. We decided that it was best for baby to come out fully undrugged and aware. We wanted to be fully present and not knocked into a state of unconsciousness when our precious ones were born. And so it would be for me. It was a bunch of crap, but I bought into the idea. It is the right thing for some women but for me, not so much.

Dan and I prepared. We took Lamaze classes. I learned hypnotherapy. I even had a mantra: "I am opening. The baby is coming. All is well." I had a poster board that my sister and girlfriends had painted with calming dolphins and positive messages. I was ready when the time came on March 4, 2001, and I went into labor.

When my water broke, Dan and I went to breakfast at the local diner and down to the beach for a walk. We saw dolphins and knew it was a sign that our little Jackson Blue was on his way. Within an hour I was doubled over in pain at the local mall where I went to find my "delivery" outfit. We ditched the dressing room quickly with the only nightie that fit my 192-pound frame: white jersey with red and pink hearts on it. Why we did that, I have no idea. But Dan indulged me. I needed a "look." I think I was already out of my mind.

Within two hours we were back at home and a thunderstorm had started outside that matched my insides. I spent 22 hours in that thunderstorm, with only a glass of wine to sedate me and Dan walking me up and down the stairs of our home while the bitchy midwife rolled her eyes in boredom. The candles were lit and Enya was playing. My two dearest girlfriends were there with us. One of them, the most adamant supporter of the natural birth method, made curry soup with garlic for some reason, and I threw up from the smell. By the time my mother arrived, I was 18 hours in. I had been puking and screaming, and was so bloated that she told them straightaway I should go to the emergency room. I didn't want to give up, but I couldn't wait to go into "transition."

It was perhaps the finest word I have ever heard when it finally came. "You're in transition!" "Thank the fucking Lord!" I screamed. But I remember thinking, "If you don't get this baby out of me soon, I will find the strength to get up and strangle you with the sheets."

But after an hour and a half of the worst pain of my life, my transition still didn't end. We thought I would have to be rushed to the emergency room after all. Then the midwife told me to put my hand between my legs and feel the baby's head. And I could feel it and immediately felt so much strength that in a moment I dilated fully and could start pushing. I started screaming, "Come on, Buddy, we can do it! Come on, Buddy!" And we did it. Together. I pushed down and he pushed out. And within minutes he was lying on my belly and Dan was cutting the cord. It was the greatest moment of my life. It was also the scariest moment of my life. I was so happy and so present, and so was Jack. He was so aware, so alive. He just looked around the room at my mom and his dad and my friends and me as if to say, "What's up, guys? Why are you all looking at me like that? Did something happen I don't know about?" And we laughed and cried and within an hour, he was swaddled between Dan and me in the dim light of our bedroom and we all fell asleep.

Transition is good. It means the process or a period of changing from one state or condition to another. The transition felt like the worst part when I had Jack—but the worst part led to the best part. It was painful beyond words and I thought it would never end. But it did. And the most wondrous thing happened. My boy. The pain no longer mattered. I think sometimes if I had been in a hospital with an epidural and some Valium, it would have been easier on my son. I definitely have questioned afterward the choices I made. But it was the perfect birth for him and a perfect birth for me.

I've had many instances of becoming a butterfly, but somehow I would always find myself back on the pile with the caterpillars—other mothers who question themselves as well. Some of my fellow mothers, who had been on the pile but now are flying free, have shown me that it's okay to go back and forth from the pile to the sky. To change as your child changes.

During a trip to Hawaii last year, Jack taught me a lesson. He was about to turn 13, so I wanted to do something special with him. I surprised him on New Year's Day.

Clare told him that the exterminators were coming in the morning and he had to get up at 7 A.M. so we could leave the house. We were going to have breakfast. When he walked outside, all sleepy eyed, he saw that Clare was still in her pj's but I was not. He was a bit confused and asked, "Where are we going for breakfast?" And then I said, "How about Hualalai?" His eyes popped open when we walked outside of the gate and there was a town car waiting with his luggage in it, all packed and ready to go.

Hualalai is a resort on the Big Island of Hawaii that we had gone to many times when he was younger and holds a special place in our memories. One of the first times I was there, I was pregnant with him and swam with dolphins in the open ocean. I have a photo of a mommy and baby dolphin swimming underneath my swollen belly from that day. And after a few days, I decided that Jack and I needed to find the dolphins again. So on the last day, on rough waters off the coast under a stormy sky, we took a boat out to look. After three hours, the captain said, "This never happens. We always see dolphins." I saw Jack's face drop. He had been so excited, and I felt like a failure that I had built his expectations so high.

As the boat was about to turn around, Jack's hand shot up and pointed toward a cove. "There they are!" And indeed they were. A whole "breeding" pack of moms and babies. We pulled into the crystal clear water and Jack was the first one to the back of the boat in his flippers and mask, ready to jump off. But when the gate was open, he looked back at me a bit afraid to jump in. I was right behind him, "Come on, Buddy, we can do it," I said. And we jumped in together, holding hands for a few minutes as we swam out. When we got our bearings we put our faces under the water and saw the most magical sight. There were 20 or more dolphins swimming not only underneath us but also beside us, so close that we could reach out and touch them. He jumped at first and held my hand tighter. But as he got more comfortable, he let go and started drifting farther and farther away. I would stick my head up every now and again and yell for him, always the concerned mom. And he would pop up with a smile and give me the thumbs-up. He soon started swimming with one of the dive instructors, a girl of about 17 with shiny blond hair and a beautiful spirit. I caught up to him to ask if he was okay, and with our masks under the water he gestured again with a thumbs-up, as if to say, "Yeah, Mom, don't worry, I'm fine." And he looked in the distance to the beautiful girl and started to swim away. I watched as he disappeared into the horizon.

My heart broke in that second, but I knew the rightness of it all. He did not belong to me anymore. He was his own being, swimming in the world, and having to make choices at every corner about where to swim and with whom. His father and I could guide him, but he was old enough to make his own decisions. I had to let him go. Of course I cried. I'm supposed to. I'm his mom.

He was in the midst of a transition now.

We don't always see our children as separate human beings. Jack and I are figuring out what it means to hold on and to let go. He probably knows much more about this than I will ever know. The fact that he has the confidence and the desire to strike out, on his own, means that I've done something right. I am a good enough mom for my son, and always will be.

7

AM I A HUMANITARIAN?

Deye mon gen mon, or
There are mountains beyond mountains.

Are you a person who lives to promote human welfare selflessly?

I had a mistress once. For years I thought of her every minute of every day. I would wake in the middle of the night and she was the only one I could see. I would lie awake for hours trying to think of ways to soothe her, bring her relief, and how better to love her. During the day, I spoke to her. Now, four years later, I think of her much less. But on our anniversary, January 12 of every year, there is an ache deep in my chest, and I long for her.

Let me clarify. I was introduced to her many years ago; January 12, 2010, was the day I wholeheartedly, undoubtedly fell in love with her. After that day I could no longer resist her raw beauty and violent, extreme love. She wanted me. She needed me. And I gave myself to her, not knowing that it would be the end of life as I knew it.

She was mysterious. People either loved her or hated her the first time they met her. She was dark and angry at times, but there was a softer, radiant side of her, too. Only certain people were able to see that side—and not because they looked for it. Only certain, special souls were able to hear the siren's cry of this mistress. And, as in the German myth of Lorelei, the siren lured sailors to crash on the rocks with her beauty and songs. Some survived and some did not. Those who did had a glimpse of her heaven.

For years I gave her everything of myself. And she took it. Eventually, I began to hate her—her draw, her sex, her death. She was a force I could not fight. And the only people who could help me heal from the wounds she caused were those who had been intimate with her as well. Two years in the middle of our tormented relationship, I was limping and barely breathing but still going back to her.

Haiti was my mistress.

In my life, I have been lucky enough to travel all around the world. I have seen the most beautiful and the most awful places. I have stayed in huts and palaces, dined with princes and beggars, and thought I had seen it all. That is, until I went to Haiti. I didn't know that I could be so completely taken in by a place. Maybe it was my wanderlust and need for adrenaline that made me spend so many years roaming the world as a quote-unquote "humanitarian." I was in Nicaragua after the earthquake in 1997 with my brother and a group of friends entertaining children with music, dance, toys, and much-needed laughter. I went to Bosnia during their war to work in refugee camps and talk to the women who had been victims of sexual violence. My humanitarian travels took me to Africa's many countries, and around the poorest parts of the United States. I was doing what I had always loved, fighting the bad guy, the oppressor. I was doing the work that Father Ray had taught me to do. I was sure that my career and public profile allowed me to push for real change, to get attention for the causes I believed in. So I never questioned if I was a humanitarian or not. Of course I was. And then Haiti hit me.

On the fourth anniversary of the earthquake in Haiti, the day 350,000 people died and millions were left homeless, I woke up early to take Jack, Clare, my mom, my dad, and my brother Joe to

Jack's soccer game. The game was an hour away, in the middle of nowhere.

I knew it was "the day," but was too busy, too afraid to deal with it that morning. My dear friend Bryn and I had texted over the week about the coming anniversary. I was supposed to have written a letter to the women I work with in Haiti for them to read at a memorial in the still-dilapidated palace. I was avoiding all of it.

It wasn't until Clare and I stopped to pick up lunch for everyone after the game that it hit me. I was standing in the bread aisle in the grocery store and suddenly a wave came over me. I saw in my mind all the faces I had known in Haiti, all the destruction, all the sorrow. I burst into tears.

So much loss and pain and tragedy. So many broken hearts and people. So much joy that would eventually turn to sorrow. The faces I see rushing in my head: Bryn, Paul, Father Rick, Barbara, Lolo, Caro, Danielle, Alison, Sean, Aleda, Captain, Suzanne, Rossanie, Lori, David, Dr. Reza, Patricia, Oscar, Donna, and many more. So why did I say yes to her call?

The first time my foot hit the ground in Haiti I knew I was in trouble. It was two years before the earthquake and our dear friend Paul Haggis invited my boyfriend, Bryn, and me to go to see the amazing work that his friend, Father Rick Frechette, was doing there. We've all heard the expression, "a place is just a place, after all." But I don't believe that. Haiti was like no place I've ever been, and I was glued to her from that moment on. Now my Haitian friends explain this instant connection to me, telling me that I was taken in by the voodoo goddess Erzulie. Erzulie is the mother symbol in voodoo, the caretaker and lover, but also the destroyer and protector. Whatever it was that grabbed me, I knew that I would be connected to this island forever.

I was smitten. The smell of diesel fuel and dust mixed with the sweet salt air was the same as in South Africa. And the airport, teeming with porters, aid workers, and dark faces, looked just like the airport in Zimbabwe. The heat hit me with its energy when I stepped out of customs. What I saw before me took my breath away.

Local buses buzzed around the parking lot where men grabbed at our luggage. The buses were small pickup trucks called tap-taps, covered with colorful paintings. Swirls of blue, purple, red, and yellow assaulted you, in hand-painted images of famous people or sayings. There was Aristide with his hands outstretched to poor children and a Virgin Mary who happened to look just like Erzulie. The best one I saw was a picture of Sylvester Stallone as Jesus Christ.

We rode up the hill in the back of a pickup truck on pock-marked roads teeming with people. We passed hundreds of tiny cement buildings, many wrapped in banners advertising "Lotto." It was like the buildings were wrapped in hope. These banners were everywhere. Every person in Haiti was willing to bet on becoming a millionaire, it seemed, even if they had to spend 25 cents on a ticket when they only made 2 dollars a day. There were just as many beauty salons advertising their expertise on painted portrait signs hanging outside. Beautiful, dark-, medium-, and light-faced men and women with braided, long, or short hair graced the signs, each offering a brand-new life if you went inside.

I loved the sounds of Creole spoken loudly, the laughing and the haggling at the tiny stands selling Wrigley's chewing gum, Fanta, and Coke. Art filled every corner. Paintings of Haitian women dancing, of Haitian men working the fields, wooden sculptures of entwined men and women, and colorful symbols of voodoo gods and goddesses (known as *veves*) sewn with brightly colored sequins.

A few miles farther down the road we saw rusted tin shacks and old pieces of wood heaped together to form a home for a nuclear family, extended family, a chicken, *and* a goat. The smiling children I captured on film were playing on a heap of garbage in an open sewer. Their mothers were washing their pots to cook their dinner in the same water.

We ended up hours later in Pétionville. I found myself in an entirely new landscape, one lush with vegetation, fine restaurants, and fancy homes. The traffic through the city and "up the Hill" is worse than on the 405 in LA on a Friday night. But the sights and sounds couldn't be more different. It is like driving through a carnival. At every corner, no matter which part of the town I was in, I was assaulted with joy.

After my first trip, I became obsessed with Haiti. I went a few more times to visit, and even made some great friends there. One was Father Rick, an Augustinian priest who had built the first pediatric hospital on the island and worked with the poorest of the poor. The other was Danielle Saint-Lot, a leader in women's rights activism in Haiti. They became heroes to me. And they still are.

On January 12, 2010, I was sitting in a room with a couples' counselor. Bryn and I had been seeing her for months, knowing that our romantic relationship was ending but not sure how to actually finish it. She had us draw diagrams of our "families of origin" to see why we were afraid of intimacy. She made us hold each other in a strange yoga pose and breathe together when we were in the midst of a fight. It was all pretty ineffectual, to be frank. I actually came to loathe this curly-red-haired lady with the pursed lips who dressed like a hippie. On this day, I knew it would be the last time I saw her.

I sat with her in the office alone while Bryn sat outside in the waiting room on the day we had agreed to finally break up. Bryn is truly one of the greatest men I've ever met, and our shared values of love, truth, and service drew us together, but we weren't meant to stay in our relationship as it currently existed. And though I was terrified how our breakup might affect my then eight-year-old son, who loved Bryn, I knew I was making the right choice. Our age difference and where we were in our lives made it impossible to continue our live-in romantic relationship. And he knew it, too. Right before my session ended, Bryn burst through the door. "There's been an earthquake in Haiti!" he shouted. I immediately got up and ran to his side to watch the news report on his phone. This beautiful country I loved was in ruins, her people screaming and crying.

There were 20-something of us on a plane headed to Port-au-Prince, six days after the earthquake. We were a motley crew of professional aid workers, Hollywood folks, a tugboat captain, a yoga instructor, doctors, a politician, and a woman who actually brought an entire suitcase with an espresso maker in it and another large one marked *makeup*. I can't say everyone had the same reasons for going to the disaster zone. Some were excited by the adrenaline, following disaster after disaster. Some had seen the news and knew that they had to be of service.

Looking out the window of the plane as it descended on the tarmac that day, I did not see the Haiti I knew. There was a film of yellow dust in the sky shutting out the usually bright sun. The bright blue waters of the Caribbean that I loved seeing upon my arrival were mixed with brown dirt. Everywhere buildings were half standing and destroyed. My mistress was dying.

The first night, sleeping on the ground under eucalyptus trees outside of a crumbling old house behind walls, we heard the sounds of grief on the streets. But deep in the night, two of my fellow aid workers awoke to the sound of singing just as the sun was rising. They jumped in a truck to see where it was coming from, and followed the voices to a place just up the hill—a previously beautiful golf club that was now half destroyed, with thousands of families living there under sheets. One of the most beautiful sights I have ever seen was the U.S. Army handing bags of rice down the hill in a line of 50 or so service people at sunrise, like an old-fashioned fire brigade. Below were women in a line, peacefully waiting their turn to get their bag of rice. And they were singing, like angels. When we asked our translator what they were singing, he said it was a song of gratitude for who was still alive. They could have been singing songs of grief, but instead were thanking God for the gift of life. The soldiers were like angels delivering kindness and compassion to the weak and weary.

Those of us who went in those days just after the quake all experienced a deep despair, and an incredible joy, feelings that would bond us together for life. In those first few months after the earthquake, I saw the best and worst of what human beings, nature, and I are capable of. I saw moments of grace that I won't ever forget. We were all changed by what we experienced. When I left Haiti for the first time after the earthquake, all I could think of was returning.

I put the love I had for the country into the people I met in Haiti. I spent three years pouring my heart and soul into my efforts there, and I, just like the others I worked with, held on for dear life in the face of so much need and devastation. We had our own needs, too—love, reassurance, sex at the end of the night—anything to save ourselves from giving in to the grief, salve we could put on the wounds we felt. After days of trying to get medicine to the hospital so that people didn't have to have their legs cut off without anesthesia, trying to get kids out of the country who had suffered spinal cord injuries, meeting women who were being raped in the camps, and constantly witnessing devastation of all kinds, I was exhausted in body and soul. But I couldn't help but go back. Over and over again.

I believe that if that group I worked with had not fallen in love with each other the way we did, and experienced what we did, together, most of us would have never gone back. Even I, who had such strong feelings for Haiti before the earthquake, may have stayed away. It was our love for the country, but also our dedication to each other, that kept us in her grasp.

There were many incarnations of relationships in our group—romantic, business, or platonic—that shifted and changed constantly in those years after the earthquake. We all fought and laughed and drank and made love and broke up and made up and raged and screamed at each other and at the country that seemed to have been forgotten by much of the world. I think when she started to see she was losing one of us to a simpler life away from the island, Haiti created chaos and drama between the groups to keep us there. From the hopeful, loving place where we all started, altruistic but drunk with adrenaline, we eventually ended up torn apart and displaced.

During my time in Haiti, I fell hopelessly in love with a man who became a driving force in my staying there. And I became that for him. I then developed a relationship with a woman, the beautiful Lolo, who first captivated me with her golden eyes and confident stare. Haiti was a place where emotions came rushing forward—your heart was raw and open to feeling at all times.

I met people who became dear friends, like family even. My wide array of friends included powerful Haitian artists and activists such as the incredible badass Barbara Guillaume. Barbara can call one person and within an hour the entire country will know what she said. Other friends of mine were from the well-to-do families in Haiti who had left seeking a better life, but came home to help when disaster struck. This was the case for Caroline Sada, who, once she returned after the quake, drove down to the neighborhoods of Cité Soleil and asked the pastor of the ruined church what he needed. Five years later, she and the pastor have built a school, a playground, and businesses that have transformed the community. I am in awe of these people and will be for the rest of my life.

One of the other remarkable things that happened in Haiti was the way "Hollywood folks" showed up. People often ask if the celebrities, including myself, were there for the right reasons. Were we just trying to get good press and prove to the world what great people we were? The truth is, all of the celebrities I knew who worked in the country long term were there from a place of deep compassion and a desire to make change. And they all have, in very powerful and profound ways, but all very differently.

As we began to think about how to raise awareness of the dire situation in the country, my colleagues and I did not agree on how to most effectively involve celebrities in the cause. Some said that we should just take these high-profile folks to the areas most broken and show them what needed to be fixed, have a camera on hand to capture them holding a suffering baby, and put it out to the world. And that method worked. Imagine how great a young, self-involved, and very famous musician felt when he went to Haiti for two days and held the hand of a little girl who was being operated on after a rape. He felt good, and so gave money to the organization that had helped the girl, thus bringing attention to the work the organization was doing.

Others, including myself, had a different approach. We wanted to show the world how Haitians were rebuilding their *own* country. One shining example of this was the trade and fashion show that many of the Haitian women I worked with put together. Just one year after the earthquake, they were designing, manufacturing, and distributing their goods to the world. I wanted the world to see what smart support and investment could do to help make this country stronger and more resilient. When I brought people to the country, specifically celebrities, I didn't want them to meet only the people in need. Many others were raising awareness for those people. I needed the celebrities to know Haiti's change makers and influencers, people invested in rebuilding a stronger and more resilient country, and to know that Haiti was looking forward, to the future. By focusing my efforts on celebrating the most powerful, my feeling was that we could do more to help those most in need.

This strategy was not without its challenges. It was a tense, then awful, then funny few days when I brought a couple of very kind and well-intentioned celebrities to see how Haiti was recovering a year after the earthquake. They arrived late one night to discover that their nice hotel did not serve food after 9 P.M. Since many of us there were hardened relief workers, the thought hadn't occurred to us that maybe these two might need some additional TLC on their first night in a new country. Instead, we threw some energy bars at them with an air of "good luck and see you in the morning!" The next night, while driving in an armored car, a canister of pepper spray accidentally went off and one of the lovely celebrities was literally choking, eyes burning in pain. To her credit, she had a great sense of humor about the whole thing.

Then, after taking them to a clinic where we bathed 100 kids in the same pool, with only one towel to dry them, they were close to leaving. But things became even more tense when we took them to the mansion of the cousin of the president for a big party, with a traditional Haitian band playing. The famous folks were righteously indignant, as they had come to Haiti to hold orphaned babies, not go to parties. But the people there were talking about investment and tourism and rebuilding and had the influence to make these ideas real, and they were who I wanted these famous folks to meet. And for the Haitians who were present that night with the celebrities, they were inspired to see such famous people in their home showing concern about their country. Many said that after, they felt a renewed sense of energy to rebuild a better Haiti and to keep fighting. I like to think that after everything, the celebrities were grateful to have experienced such a range of emotions and to have seen the full array of what Haiti was.

A group of women and I started the organization We Advance. Our mission started in a tiny yellow clinic in Cité Soleil, the poorest slum in the Western Hemisphere. The neighborhood of tin shacks was like the film set of the dirtiest, most devastating place you could ever imagine, with its cesspools filled with rotten water and trash where the children bathed. Out of the "Sunshine Clinic" we put Band-Aids wherever they were needed, whether that meant giving out medicine, giving a mother food for her baby, or helping a rape victim. Eventually we realized there were never going to be enough hands or enough Band-Aids. What the women really needed and wanted was an education so that they could help themselves. That network is up and running as We Advance University, the first online educational site for women's groups all over the country. We are still struggling for funding, but it is my great hope we will stay up and running.

When we needed a break from the Sunshine Clinic, we would head to the beach in Jacmel. It is on the other side of the island from Port-au-Prince, an area that most people never see. It is paradise on earth. On our days away from the disaster of the city, we would drive through the slums, up to the heavenly mountain pass leading to a town that looked like New Orleans. With its artisans and architecture, with interesting people from all over the world, Jacmel held the promise of what Haiti could be.

On one particular weekend I drove with friends to Jacmel. I was tired from working at the clinic, my leadership skills questioned, even by myself. I was getting over a relationship that I had enjoyed, but knew had to end. As soon as we arrived at the simple but elegant hut on the beach that belonged to our hosts, I dove into the crystal blue waters with all of my clothes on. I wanted to be healed and to wash away the pain that was hanging off me from the city. We all needed to be cleansed. But the truth is, it got harder and harder to feel clean as time went by.

We all hung on as long as possible, sometimes our egos the only thing driving us to stay. Bryn later said that one of the reasons he lived in a tent for two years in Haiti while working at the hospital and building a school was because he was trying to prove that he could, to others, to himself, and to me. And what was I trying to prove? That I could make a difference? That my voice mattered? That I could convince the world to listen to the women of this great country? That I was a humanitarian?

I think if I were a true "humanitarian," I would have stayed longer, and continued to go back even if almost everyone who I knew and loved had gone. If I were a true humanitarian by the definition—"a person who seeks to promote human welfare"— maybe I would be living in Cité Soleil now. An antonym for *humanitarian* is *selfish*. The truth was, I wanted to give relief because I also needed relief.

I tried as hard as I could to hold on. I think now that I failed miserably. I was foolish in the way I walked in Haiti, with bare feet in the slums, washing children in a dirty pool. I was rewarded with hundreds of parasites that tried to eat me alive. But would I take it back? Could I ever forget the smell, the life, the resilience, the sex, and the generosity? Never.

So no, I would not consider myself a humanitarian. Nor would I consider myself selfish. I would label myself a "human," trying to do my best in this beautiful fucked-up world to make a difference, for this country I love, for my friends, and for myself. As they say, time does heal wounds, and Haiti has proven she is more resilient than I could have imagined.

I will be back soon, my love.

8

AM I CINDERELLA?

Is there a "sole mate" out there for you?

On a freezing cold, snowy night in December 1992, I was walking in New York City. After a year of taking acting classes I was finally getting auditions, mostly for commercials and small plays. It was around 5 P.M. and the snow was just beginning to hit the ground. I was excited, and said affirmations to myself for twelve blocks. (Those were the days when affirmations were becoming popular.)

"I am a big famous movie star."

"This part is mine under divine grace."

"I am living my dream."

I smiled the whole way, desperately wanting my affirmations to work. My manager had explained that the audition I was headed to was for a "big Hollywood movie." This was the most important one I'd ever been on.

When I got to the audition, there were already six other women sitting in a tiny room, waiting to be seen. I immediately became deflated. I sensed that all the other pretty blond-haired actresses had done their affirmations as well. Mine stopped working for me the minute I realized this. But I sucked it up and went into the room with the casting director and the reader.

I want to explain a little bit more about the auditioning process. When an actor goes for an audition, you often wait for hours in what feels like, and sometimes looks like, a holding cell. When your number (or name) is called, you take the long walk to the courtroom where the jury will tell you if you are good or bad. That jury will consist of a casting director, a camera person, and a reader. If you are lucky and the casting director is good, the reader will be a fellow actor who performs the scene with you as you look into a camera. But sometimes, the reader is the assistant of the main assistant who just sits there, saying the lines that come before and after yours.

This audition consisted of a scene in which my father has just died. The scene started with me speaking to my mother with a defensive tone, and ended with me breaking down in the corner as she held me. In this instance, the mother was played by a 50-year-old man who had never acted in his life, but was capable of chewing gum and drinking coffee at the same time. Regardless, I thought I did great. Even the female casting director said as much.

So I said a series of affirmations of gratitude all the way back to my tiny apartment on Christopher Street.

"I am so grateful for this opportunity to be in this movie."

"My time has come, and so it is done."

"I draw people toward me who help realize my dream."

No sooner than I had opened the door, I heard the phone ringing. (I know it's hard to believe that there was a time when you actually had to be home for a phone call!) "Oh, that must be a good sign," I thought. "They only call so quickly when they want you!"

It was my manager. The next moments are a blur, but as best I can remember he said, "Well, the casting director said, and I quote, you 'need to go back to school and learn how to act. And don't send her on any more auditions until she does.'"

"Oh," he added, "she called your agents to tell them, too, and they totally agree. They've fired you."

After hanging up, I sat crying and devastated in my roach-infested apartment. Eventually, I ran down the stairs and I just started walking. By the time I got to 23rd Street, dressed in my army boots and black leather jacket, I was ranting to God in my head. "Okay, God, what are you trying to tell me? That this is it? I guess I'm not supposed to be an actress. The casting directors, my agents, they are all right. I don't know how to act and I never will no matter how many classes I take. I'm going back to Philly and starting over."

Without thinking, I just kept walking straight ahead against the cold wind. Suddenly, something caught my eye. I caught a glint of light coming from the snow, outside of a gray stone building. I went over to see what it was. It was a shoe. Not just any shoe. It was a golden, glittery pump. And what did this Cinderella do? She sat down in the snow on 23rd Street, took off her black army boot, and put the gold shoe on. And it fit. Perfectly.

"Thank you, God," I said over and over again. "Thank you for this sign." I just knew that he was telling me that I was on the right path and to stay the course. I took that golden shoe as a gift. It would be with me for almost 20 years. That shoe would travel from New York to LA and back again. Whenever I got depressed, I would look at it and remember how it had been delivered as a sign to tell me that I was supposed to keep going. I was supposed to be acting.

Over the years, my friends and family loved to laugh at me, because I would look for signs everywhere. Of course I don't always find them, but I do believe there are signs out there for all of us. My mom taught my siblings and me this when we were kids. Whenever Mom was in a tough situation, a rose would appear. She said it was a sign from Mary that all would be well, and most of the time she was right. "Signs are everywhere," she said. "We just have to keep our eyes, ears, and hearts open for them."

But now there's something I need to confess, something I learned to do well during all those years in Catholic school. For me, that shoe was not just a sign that I should continue acting. It was my missing glass slipper. I believed, until an embarrassingly adult age, that I would find the Prince Charming who went along with that shoe. Yes, I had Prince Charming Syndrome. I don't think that is an approved mental illness by the American Psychiatric Association, but it should be, because I think many of us suffer from it.

I always believed that my Prince Charming was coming. I searched my whole life for a match to my shoe, waiting for some prince to show up with it in his hands. I met so many princes along the way. Some of them acted quite princely. Some of them even looked quite princely. Some of them *were* princely. But most of the princes I found in my 20s and 30s were just the same guy over and over, with a different name.

Here's a snapshot of some of my princes.

The first I'll call Prince Charmingly Unconscious. He would express his love for me only when he was on Vicodin.

The day after we slept together, I called him. He didn't call back the next day, or the day after that. And for a month, I lay in bed despondent. I listened to Sarah McLachlan's album *Mirrorball* and the song "Hold On" over and over, and I cried like a baby.

I was devastated when, shortly after, a tabloid ran a story about him hooking up with a 20-something stripper and getting sent to rehab for prescription drug addiction. He looked bloated and dissipated in the photo. "See," I thought to myself, "if he had only given in to his love for me, he would be so much better. I know he had had intimacy issues, but if I had only stuck around long enough, I could've helped him break through them."

The second, Prince Bad Charming, told me on the first night we met that he was a "man of bad character," a player, and had just had a threesome in Montreal with two friends or two hookers, I can't remember anymore. He said what he liked about the threesome was that the other two didn't need him, that they were quite happy without him. A therapist might have said that he was a voyeur, enjoying the others' pleasure of each other, and enjoying the bizarre validation he got from being reminded that he wasn't really needed or wanted.

He told me after a couple of hours of talking that he was never this open with anyone. He told me that he either had a connection with a woman or else he wanted to have sex with her. Now he was stuck, because we seemed to have this mystical connection *and* he wanted to sleep with me. So, what did I think?

"Yes! The real Prince Charming has arrived!" was what I thought. Of course.

Our first kiss happened that very first night and I was sure I was in love. It had been a long time since I'd felt the exhilaration of that sort of physical and (I thought) spiritual connection, and though he told me outright that he was nearly incapable of intimacy, I believed, of course, he could change. Of course I did. In my head I knew that I was being a foolish woman and that he certainly would not change. But my little girl heart so wanted it to be true.

A few days later we met for dinner with a small group. I was a little drunk and decided to be the first one to leave. As I got up, in my skintight black skirt and four-inch heels, and made my way around the table, kissing everyone good-bye, my prince said,

"I'll walk you out and get you a cab." I knew what this meant. I had been thinking of kissing him all night. I was even more drawn to him since he had been so vulnerable with me the other day, sharing his story of his days as a drug addict. He was more damaged than I could have imagined.

He took me over to some bushes behind the restaurant, threw me against the wall, and started kissing me ferociously. It was a blurry haze of hands and tongues. Suddenly, he stopped.

"What's going on here?" he asked.

I was out of breath. "What do you mean? We're kissing, we like each other, and we're single. What could be wrong with this?"

And as his sexual energy subsided, he put his hands on his head and said, "I'm not actually single."

I was dumbfounded. "But you told me just three weeks ago that you were single! How the hell did you get a girlfriend in three weeks, especially after the way we kissed at my house? Are you out of your mind?" Now I was fuming but, not surprisingly, even more turned on.

"Remember the girl I told you about, my friend? Well, we decided to give it a go. She is a great person, and I'm not that sexually into her, but she's my best friend, so what do you think?"

"So break up with her," I almost yelled.

Sweet tortured soul said, "I can't."

I was officially devastated but managed to say, "Then don't kiss me anymore."

I turned away, jumped in a cab, and left him staring longingly after me with sad actor eyes. It was a classic scene from a bad romantic comedy.

Naturally it didn't end there. A few weeks later, after daily make-out sessions, I finally decided to sleep with him. I wore a slip dress with knee-high stockings. I was ready for sexy, loving sex. After his hourly texts expressing his deep love and appreciation for me, it seemed he was ready as well. I fantasized that he would meet me at the door and we would pounce on each other and make love. Then we would hold each other for a while and afterward eat Chinese takeout from cartons and laugh while we lie in bed naked. It was another scene I'd written in my head for the romantic comedy I was hoping to star in opposite him.

Instead, I found him having a massage when I opened his door. I hung out on his balcony for an hour until he was done getting poked and prodded. I wanted to leave. I knew that if I had more self-respect, I would have left. But my anxiety had been spiked and my brain was not working properly.

When the masseuse left, I silently made my way to the white couch in his living room. While he checked his messages to see how his next movie was coming along, I stared at the coffee table in front of me and saw a greeting card from his girlfriend. It declared, "My undying love and affection." I got a glimpse of the inside and saw that the writing was like that of a high school girl, complete with hearts over the *i*'s.

"She has it worse than me," I thought. And at least he wasn't lying to me about who he was. But then, the emotionally adolescent part of me thought, "Oh God, he loves her more." I got more and more depressed sitting there.

Instead of my well-written love scene, we ended up having brief sex on the couch. Suffice to say, he was satisfied. When I pretended to be "satisfied," he leapt off the couch to his computer. I was sweaty and my creamy-white slip dress torn. I was mortified. He called out to me, and of course I ran to him.

I went over to his chair and I tried to embrace him. Seriously, yes, I tried. He told me about his upcoming movie and showed me screenshots of his oiled abs and scruffy, mean-looking face. He said that this film would make him a full-blown movie star, as he took me painstakingly through every scene. He then showed me fan mail from various women around the world. He was so proud. I was both disgusted and jealous in equal amounts.

Finally, I got a hold of myself, popped up, and said, near tears, "I am in so much pain right now."

He looked at me and asked, "What's wrong, baby? Do you need an aspirin?"

And this just about sums up the depth of our emotional connection. An aspirin.

Another prince was actually a bit closer to "princely" than the others. Our relationship began in a magical place, with him riding in on his white horse to save me and the world. He asked me to marry him before we had even kissed. He was obviously looking for a princess of his own, a woman to save him and tell him he was a good guy. Three months later we were screaming and throwing steaks at each other's heads and he was telling me what a "fuckup" I was.

All three of these men were figments of my imagination, just characters in my play. I had cast myself as Cinderella, hoping my Prince Charming would notice me and choose me as his special one. I actually thought every one of these men was my soul mate. Now I see how delusional I was, and how I debased myself when I should have known better. It embarrasses me, in some ways, to even remember the way I behaved. And yet the lessons I learned from each of these relationships were life changing. I realized that I "made people up." I had a fantasy in my mind of who each of these men was, even when I didn't really know any of them.

I've seen these guys in tabloids over the years. One of them turned out to be a lonely, addicted, unhappy, not-so-good-looking man who barely worked again. The other looks the same, except he's orange, because he's become addicted to the fake tanner he's been using for years. And the third one, well, he's still out there looking.

As much as I do enjoy a good vengeful laugh about my fictional princes, I see now that they were lonely and afraid, too, needing validation as much as I did. They needed to know that they were famous enough, rich enough, and good enough to be wanted by every woman they met. I can't say I wasn't looking for the same. We were all dancing to the same music. I felt like a victim of their neuroses at the time, but, in fact, I was just as neurotic as they were.

The names and circumstances have been changed to protect the guilty. So don't try and guess who these guys are. Besides, who they are is not important. They're really just one big mashup of variations on a theme: handsome, self-involved, with a heap of hopes and dreams projected onto them by me.

I wanted to be special. I thought when I became the *one* all of my anxiety would disappear and then I would be someone. These bad princes were not going to do that for me. But I eventually learned that not even the good princes could.

I was lucky to have a few good princes in my life. Men who held me when I felt I was broken, made me laugh, understood me, and showed me all of themselves. Thank God the father of my child is one of the good ones. But, even still, no one could help fill the hole that I felt was inside of me. I was on an endless search for the mate to my golden shoe.

My first golden shoe, the one I had found on the street in New York City as a young woman, brought me luck—from being cast on *ER*, then in *Payback, Coyote Ugly, The Cooler, A History of Violence,* and others that came after. One day during the acceptance of an award in San Francisco, I thought about my old shoe. I thought about how all the dreams I had connected to that talisman had come true. I was by then a working actress, acknowledged for taking challenging roles. I was a mother of a really great kid. I realized, while I was giving the speech, that the shoe had given me everything I asked for and more. I decided to tell the crowd the story of my magic shoe and decided the time had come for me to pass the shoe on to another Cinderella, someone else who needed dreams.

And I did.

Not long afterward, in the midst of yet another breakup, I went to New York to make a film. I brought my golden shoe. It was springtime and the cherry blossoms were out in Sheep's Meadow in Central Park. I went with my golden shoe in hand to lie in the green grass. I was wondering what I should do with my shoe. I took out my phone and started to photograph it. First in the grass, then in my hand, and finally near the big tree I used to sit under when I was a struggling actress right off the bus from Philly. I realized the moment had come to let it go.

I went back to my room and wrote my story on two sheets of paper. I didn't put my name on it, but explained the story of the shoe and how it had brought me luck and given me the courage to walk on no matter what. I wrote that the key was to stand on your own feet, in your own shoes, and not wait for Prince Charming or Cinderella to kneel before you with arms outstretched so that you could succeed.

I put the shoe on a piece of old cardboard outside of the front door of the hotel. I wrote in big letters "IF you are a size 9 please try me on, if not keep walking." I put the note underneath the shoe and I made the doormen promise to keep an eye on it. A few minutes later I got in my car to go to the airport. I turned around and watched my shoe till it was out of sight and then I started bawling my eyes out. The kind driver asked me if I was okay and I told him my story. He said something like "It was very brave of you to let it go. Remember, what you give, you get back tenfold."

I probably will never know who has that magic shoe, but I hope they were inspired by it as much as I was. I hope they are flying right now and following their dreams.

A couple of months later back in LA, Jackson, Milo, and I were walking on the beach with Milo's mom, Camryn Manheim. Milo and Jackson were born one day apart and they are like brothers. Camryn has scraped me off the floor many times when I was having a breakdown about my child, my love life, and life in general. She is one of the most practical and generous people I know. As we walked on the beach that day, with the boys running ahead of us playing on the jetty and in the surf, I was content. Then Jackson came running back to me. He was holding something in his hand. "Mom, Mom, look! I found your gold shoe!" He was holding an old beat-up golden ballet slipper. Camryn knew the story of my shoe as well so we all just sat there in awe. I brought it home, of course.

A month later I was walking out of the Hollywood Bowl with my then boyfriend, Bryn. After a few blocks I looked down to step around an object on the dark pavement in front of me and stopped in my tracks. It was a gold spray-painted UGG. I picked it up. A few feet later, another object blocked my path: it was a gold sneaker. And there was another and another and another. In all I picked up five gold shoes! I learned later that on the bottoms of the shoes were stickers with an advertisement for an art show. It didn't matter to me. It was another sign. I now had six gold shoes. The driver was right, I gave something away out of love, and it came back to me more than I could ever imagine. The shoes now sit on a shelf in my living room next to the photo of my old gold shoe.

I will never stop looking for golden shoes—signs that I am on the right path. But I have stopped looking for someone else to deliver the "missing one" to my door. I just bought myself a pair of gold peep-toe pumps at DSW that fit me perfectly!

That's the thing about shoes. Only you know how they fit. No one can tell you how they actually feel or just how far you can walk in them. Seems to me, if you wait for some prince or princess to come along and deliver them, you'll be waiting forever.

So I'm passing on my shoes to you, in the form of lessons that have changed me. I have finally stopped waiting for someone to bring me my lost shoe. Oddly enough it was my father who helped me see this most clearly. He was never the Prince Charming many young girls expect their fathers to be. Quite the contrary. But later in life, as we healed our relationship, he helped me see that he and my mother had already given me the pair of golden shoes that I would never lose.

My own two feet.

9

AM I DAMAGED?

It wasn't until the late 1980s, when Oprah came on television, that we discovered my father had bipolar disorder. When my father was growing up, and even when I was growing up, people who seemed strange, agitated, or not quite there were labeled "crazy." I remember going to Norristown State Mental Hospital when I was a Girl Scout to give cookies to the patients. I will never forget the smell of urine and the chorus of screams. I will never forget the poor man lying on his side in a pile of his own feces. I wondered what was so wrong with him that he had to live there. I now wonder why the head of our Girl Scouts troop thought it was a good idea to bring young girls to a place like that.

When we were children we didn't know that in addition to being addicted to alcohol and drugs, my father was also bipolar. He would rage and hit and scream, and then sometimes was not able to get out of bed for days on end. Still other times there were moments of sanity and kindness. And yet, through it all, we believed that my dad was a good man with a kind heart, a behavior our mother modeled for us. We saw his hurt through our own pain and often sympathized with him.

After my father broke his back he was labeled "a cripple." Now we call it "handicapped." But the worst part is that it wasn't because he was physically disabled that he went off the rails. From a very early age, my dad showed signs of what we now know as bipolar disorder. The beast was always there. His injury just unlocked the cage.

My father wishes that he had gone to college at 17, instead of joining the army. Back in the 1950s, they didn't have diagnoses like ADD or ADHD, so my dad was just labeled "a troubled, dumb kid." Even his parents told him so. But he was curious. He wanted to learn. He could have done great things had he believed in himself, and understood himself more.

From the onset of puberty, I would become possessed by rages and depression. I contemplated and staged my suicide at age 12. I wrote about it in my pink Holly Hobbie diary, which I locked with a key. I'm sad I don't have that journal now, but I remember every moment of the evening.

I was 12 years old, living in my suburban Philadelphia neighborhood. I was five five, the tallest kid in my sixth grade class. I weighed about a buck forty. I was not a little girl. My house was in chaos. Some months before, my dad had been taken away to rehab after he had destroyed the house and the hearts of those of us inside, yet again. When he got back after a few months, he seemed okay, but out of it. Since he was off painkillers, he was in agony every minute. Of course that made him depressed. How could it not? And when he got depressed, instead of going inside of himself and putting his head under the covers, as I did, he would lash out. I tried everything I could to flee that house.

I was in love with Robbie, a boy in my older brother's class. After school some days, I would sneak out of our house if my dad was passed out, on the pretense of walking my dog, Coco, and steal looks at Robbie riding his little Honda 85 motorbike. I fantasized that he'd stop one day, hold out his hand, and ask me to ride. I'd hop on back, throw my arms around him, and we'd jet away like Aidan Quinn and Daryl Hannah in *Reckless*. I'd never have to go back home. I would be saved. I heard Robbie liked me, too, so I went out walking every day for two months. He would talk to me in his shy way with his bike revving high and then ride away without asking me to hop on. Soon, I thought. Soon.

A week before Christmas a public school girl had a party. I was invited and so was Robbie. I knew it would be the night that we would kiss. He would hold me and we would fall in love. We had a connection. I was sure that he was my soul mate.

I arrived at the party in my new Christmas clogs and my cool green corduroy "horse pants," as I called them, since they had a label with a horse on them. I didn't know then they were Levi's. When I got to the party I felt quite shy, but I held my head high, walked down to the basement, and looked for my man. When my eyes adjusted to the blackness, I saw a swarm of people slow dancing to "Stairway to Heaven." I imagined I'd find him alone in the crowd and we'd begin a slow, sweet dance that culminated in a kiss. Pushing through the crowd I found him in a corner making out with the party girl's cousin. Tongues everywhere. Before I knew what I was doing, I grabbed the black-haired ninth grade girl whom he was kissing by the hair and pulled her off him. Then I pushed him and ran back up the stairs.

Everyone had stopped to stare and now they rushed up the stairs after me. The cousin was right on my back, and before I reached the driveway, she turned me around and slapped me, all the kids looking on. "You crazy bitch! What the fuck do you think you're doing! You're fucking crazy!" she screamed. The mother of the party girl came out and yelled at me to leave. I started walking away toward a smirking Robbie and he promptly tripped me. When I was on the ground he chuckled and said, "You are really fucked up." Laughter all around. I got up and walked home. I had broken my new clogs. I had a rip in the knee of my new horse pants. I was humiliated.

I went home to bed, stuck my head under a pillow, and cried for the next two days as I planned my suicide. I cried because no one would ever want me, because I was too messed up. And now, everyone knew. They knew that my father was sick in his head and that I was just like him.

The day of Christmas Eve, after helping my mom peel the potatoes and clean the celery and radishes for that night's feast, I went to my room and began to write in my little diary:

> *Dear Diary,*
> *Today will be the last day of my life. Tonight after*
> *6 o'clock mass, I will not stay with the rest of my*
> *family for cookies and coffee in the hall with the other*
> *parishioners. I will pretend to be sick. I will walk home.*
> *I will go upstairs to my father's armoire where he keeps*
> *his magazines and his guns. I will take out the little*

gun and go to my room. I will hold the gun to my head
and pull the trigger. I will die. Robbie will know I love
him. My parents will be sad. I will never have to face my
classmates again. I will be so happy.

Love,

Maria

P.S. The only way I won't follow through with my plan is
if it snows tonight by the time I get out of church. Then
it will be a sign from God that I am not supposed to kill
myself. Thanks.

I don't know why I wrote that P.S., but I did. It was a particularly mild December and we had seen no snow that winter. There were no signs in the forecast, either. I suppose I was looking for a miracle, like the virgin birth and those three kings following a star to find the stable in Bethlehem where a king would be born. How did they know which star to follow, anyway? That was definitely a miracle. So, if God really wanted me to keep on living my lousy life, if he wanted me to go on living with the knowledge that I was a monster, if he wanted me to suffer for the next seven years until I could get out of this house, then he'd send me a miracle, too. He'd send a little snow.

I dressed for the occasion of my death. I wore my maroon, flowered Laura Ingalls dress, a two-inch heel from Sears, my mom's pantyhose, and my long bleached blond tresses hanging down my back except for a tiny braid off to the left side. I walked up to the tiny church with my brothers and sister. I wore no coat because it was nearly 68 degrees. We walked in silence.

During mass, I thought of little else but my death. I realized that in a few days, all of these people would be gathered again to mourn at my funeral. All the girls from my class who had stopped playing with me because I hung out with the younger Marianne Murray, the mean Sister Michael, and, of course, Robbie (who would be devastated) would all be there. My mom and dad, grandmas and grandpas, and siblings would all be in the front row sobbing.

When mass was over and it was time to walk outside, I stopped behind the closed wooden doors and let the others go ahead to the hall. This was it. I was ready. I looked back at the altar. The smell of frankincense hung in the air. Good-bye, God, old friend, see you soon. I walked out with my eyes closed.

I felt a tiny wetness on my face. I opened my eyes to a sprinkling of little white flakes that vanished as soon as they hit the ground. It was snowing! Kinda sorta. Thank you, God! I was overjoyed. Not to be spared death, but because someone was finally listening. It was a miracle. My own little Christmas Eve miracle, just for me.

I would contemplate suicide many times after that. I thought that something from my childhood had broken me in such a way that I could not survive. I tried to cure myself of the pain by latching on to spiritual healers and spending hours with therapists.

Most people just thought I was a deep kid. During high school, college, and my years acting in New York City, I was plagued with pain, depression, rages, and manias. And yet my friends accepted me exactly how I was. In some instances I could see myself from the outside and agreed that I had value, that I was sane. And then in the next minute I would fall down into a ditch of despair. Then, after a few days in bed, I was fine again. Until the next time.

Right before I moved to LA, a magical thing happened. In the midst of a depression, which left me terrified to be in groups of people, I had to cater a fancy party. As I served the mushroom tarts and then went in the kitchen to try not to cry, a man approached me. He told me he was a painter and asked me if he could paint me. I said, "Yeah right, you want me to be naked or something?" He said no, I could pose however I liked and that he would pay me $100 an hour. When I asked him why he wanted to paint me, he said, "I've never seen anyone more on the verge of insanity as you."

I took the job, sitting in a little studio on the Upper East Side for six weeks. I posed on a tiny bed, looking out of a small window onto a tree as he painted me. I really felt that with every brushstroke, he was taking a bit of the depression from me. The top of the canvas where he started was dark and moody, but as the days went on, the painting got lighter, and I, too, started to feel lighter. By the time I left, I felt solid again. It was the ultimate demonstration that art heals.

When Jackson was one, I met the kind painter by chance in an elevator in New York City. He remembered me and was happy for my success. He sent me the painting and it's hanging in my bedroom. It always reminds me of my shadow and that there is always a way to heal.

When I was 27, I moved to Los Angeles and my career quickly took off. Within a short time, I was cast in a great show. It was exhilarating and painful all at once. But I could no longer contain the pressure. As wonderful as it all was, I was bleeding inside. My emotions were out of control and I was terrified. I spent days alone in bed. I would show up for work and pretend my way through the day, thinking only, "Don't cry, don't let them see you cry." I would then hide in my trailer and cry. And then I'd come back out again. I convinced myself that people on the show didn't like me. I tried to protect myself by being distant and hard. It came off as arrogant and aloof instead. I was locked inside of my own head and couldn't get out.

On the last day of the season, I left the set quickly and jumped in my Jeep in the middle of the day and started to cry. My eyes poured big, huge tears of rage. I didn't know where I was going. I just remember being stuck in traffic during a thunderstorm and seeing a man doing push-ups in the rain beside his stalled clunker. Hours later I was on a desert road. I remember the light was a vivid blue even in the middle of the night. I had stopped crying and began saying the Hail Mary over and over again.

I finally ended up at a motel at a truck stop in Arizona. I wasn't sure how I was going to kill myself, but I knew that the time had come. As I lay curled up on the floor, wrapped in an orange-and-brown comforter, my mind cleared for a minute. This was not me, I thought. There is something wrong. Don't listen to yourself. Then I called my best friend and she called my therapist. Soon people arrived to take me home.

The next day, a kind psychiatrist in LA said, "Maria, if you are nearsighted, you need glasses to see. You have a chemical imbalance and taking medicine is like having glasses." I was quickly diagnosed with bipolar disorder. It is hereditary in some circumstances and so was true with me.

Next came three painful months of trying different combinations of drugs. The first two weeks were the worst as I waited for the drugs to take effect. My mother came out to stay with me and held my feet all night, as they couldn't stop moving. Some days I could not even speak. I was nearly comatose. A psychiatric nurse stayed at our house and made me walk every day. My brother, who was living with me at the time, cooked for me and kept his promise to let no one know what had happened to me.

After three long months, I finally found the right regimen and felt like the best of me. I could walk again. I could see clearly. I worried if the drugs would dull who I really was, take away that passion and angst and everything that made me such a good actor. Funny enough, I did my best acting roles and even won awards after the medication.

I left my first big job after those three months. I told myself I needed to heal, and to learn to cope with the triggers that might send me into fight-or-flight mode again, at any time. Then and even some years later, people may have thought I had left that job because I was arrogant—that I was bored and wanted to "do more" with my career.

I have looked back on my decision many times, getting to the heart of why I really left. As I learned more about my disease, I realized that the truth is that leaving had nothing to do with arrogance or lack of humility. At the time, in the baby stages of my recovery, my illness might have driven me to suicide if I had stayed. I finally have peace about that time, knowing that I did the right thing for my health and my future.

NOW AND AGAIN OVER THE YEARS I'VE HAD TO ADJUST MY MEDS, just like my dad and others I know who have this or similar illnesses. I am dutiful about taking my pills every day. But once every couple of years, if I am triggered in some way or the medicine stops working, I find I'm not quite myself. I know it's time to go back to the doctor. And I do. I know that without medication I would end up suicidal and eventually dead.

Of course I research constantly and read every book I can about my disease. Yes, bipolar is a disease, just like diabetes or asthma. My favorite book about depression has come to be a lifesaver when I am in my darkest days. It is William Styron's *Darkness Visible*. Styron wrote the book when he was actually in the midst of a depression and therefore captured the feeling perfectly. It is not sadness. It is not pain. It is something like a complete despair after losing your whole family in a car accident, even though the reality is that your family is just fine.

Another book that has helped me to embrace the label of bipolar was Kay Redfield Jamison's memoir *An Unquiet Mind*. In this amazing book, she writes,

Life is too complicated, too constantly changing, to be anything but what it is. . . . . It is, at the end of the day, the individual moments of restlessness, of bleakness, of strong persuasions and maddened enthusiasms, that inform one's life, change the nature and direction of one's work, and give final meaning and color to one's loves and friendships.

No matter my meds, I will always have a hypersensitivity to life. The highs and lows are somehow much higher and lower for me than for some other human beings. But I have accepted that I cannot change something that will always be a part of me. I now look at it dead in the eye without shame or judgment. And I'm lucky enough to have found kind people and medicine that keep me alive and tethered to this earth.

Just recently, I admitted on an insurance claim for a film that I was on medication for bipolar disorder. I had hidden this for years, only ever admitting on forms like these that I took Synthroid for the thyroid disease I also have. But this time I added bipolar disorder. I wanted to see what would happen. Within a few days, my lawyer received a letter asking me to sign a waiver stating that I would "take all psychiatric medicine as prescribed." We said, "No." It took weeks of negotiating to compose a letter that simply said, "I will take ALL medication prescribed during shooting." That meant my Synthroid, too. We would not allow the backers of this film to get away with putting mental disabilities in a different category from physical disabilities. In the end our argument worked and the studio agreed.

I have never missed a day of work in my life, whether from physical or mental illness. Why should I have to sign this piece of paper? Turns out that on this particular film set, one of the producers had glaucoma, the makeup artist had cancer, and someone else had a child who was showing signs of schizophrenia. So I guess we are all damaged in our ways. We all have our disabilities. I don't want to have to sign a paper vouching for mine.

Mental illness has become more acceptable now. People talk about it and "come out about it" more. And yet still there is a stigma attached. Jamison wrote another book called *Touched with Fire*. That book is about centuries of artists who would now be considered bipolar or schizophrenic. At the time, if they were diagnosed at all, these figures were labeled "hysterical." Many killed themselves. Ernest Hemingway, Virginia Woolf, Sylvia Plath, and the list goes on. I wish there had been medication for these tortured souls, so that we would have much more of their art to enjoy today.

But mental illness can also be a gift. I even enjoy being around people with "mental disorders" of some kind or other. I have a great producer friend who admittedly has Asperger's syndrome. He is on medication, but still can't stay on track for very long during a multiparty conversation. Yet he is ridiculously successful and fascinating, and has a brilliant mind.

So am I damaged? Of course, I'm human. Who isn't damaged in some way? But I'm not damaged because of my bipolar disease. Now that I am being treated, I can view it more as a gift. The wiring of my brain allows me to feel deeply. I believe it helps me be less judgmental and more empathetic to others, and certainly a better actress. And besides, it is a gift I share with my father, and millions of others all over the world.

10

AM I A FEMINIST?

Is feminism an outdated label?

In the last few years, the word *feminism* has become a very loaded term.

Some young women and even some celebrities have come out to declare that they are not feminists because feminism is divisive and "militant." Others say, well, "I am a humanist," because it seems "less threatening" and "more inclusive." Still others proudly proclaim from the global podium or from the homes they've decided to go back to after quitting their jobs to be full-time moms, "I am a feminist! Pay attention!"

The funny thing is that by claiming their own power and

expressing their opinions, even those women who claim they are not feminists are behaving like they are. They are all women who are making their own place in the world. They are not waiting for an invitation, or hoping for equality. They aren't setting the table. They are pulling up a chair and sitting at whatever table they want.

For me, calling someone a feminist is one of the highest compliments I can pay a woman, or a man, for that matter. It's a label I give myself and I wholeheartedly accept others giving it to me.

A feminist is a person who believes in the social, political, and economic equality of men and women. As Hillary Clinton said at the 1995 Beijing women's rights conference, "Women's rights are human rights."

Period. End of story.

But here's the beginning of my experiences with feminism. . . .

I wanted to play soccer in grade school. But my suburban private Catholic school did not have a girls' team. My dad, God bless him with his bad back and addictions, was the coach of my older brother's soccer team. One day when I asked him, "How come the girls don't have a team?" he shrugged his shoulders and said, "Beats the hell out of me. Just come practice with us."

By the end of the week all hell had broken loose. The priests at our church were ready to excommunicate my dad and me. And most of the fathers of the boys on the team were secretly planning to take us down, too. "There is no place for a girl in boys' sports!" they fumed. If they had been brave enough to say this to my dad's face, he would've probably beaten them all up. I'm sure my mom had something to do with keeping the priests safe from him.

Looking back on this, I now see my dad was a feminist in his way. But I didn't know it then because I had never even heard the word.

Gloria Steinem helped me understand what the word *feminist* meant. She helped everyone understand that feminism wasn't just a fad or a recent development. It's a natural part of the quest for human rights that began well before the 1960s and 1970s. As she and others explain, it started in the early 1800s in Europe when women (and some forward-thinking men) began fighting for equal property rights and the right to vote. That movement has been rolling forward ever since, though the path and the goals have changed a million ways over the years.

The first feminists I ever knew were my great-grandmother and my mom. They certainly didn't know they were feminists.

How could they? They were seemingly ordinary women of their time. But they were living extraordinary lives: raising their families on very little, securing an education despite constant resistance, and working when it was not something a woman usually did.

Babci, which is what we called my great-grandmother, never knew that she was a feminist. And Mom certainly didn't know it. Betty Friedan, Gloria Steinem, and many others shined a light on how extraordinary people like Babci and Mom really were.

Babci was born in a steel town outside of Philly to immigrant parents from Poland. She had an eighth grade education and married a Polish cobbler from her neighborhood when she was 17. By the time she was 27, she had four kids and a dead husband. They say he died of "consumption," which might have been a cover story for the real reason—that he was a drunk. One of those kids was my mother's father, PopPop Urban.

Babci was left dirt poor. Being dirt poor is exactly what it sounds like. She lived in a tiny house that had dirt floors with my grandfather and his siblings. Babci could not even afford a proper floor.

Babci's job had always been to raise her family. But now she had to go find a paying job. At the time, places like sewing mills and knitting mills were generally populated with female workers sewing uniforms for the men in World War II. The conditions were mostly deplorable, and the women made much less money than any man in the same plant. It was hard work, but Babci knew the stakes were high. Without a job, she would not be able to support her family and her kids would be taken away or worse, starve to death.

Outside of the mill, Babci was known as an excellent seamstress. Word spread of her skills, and soon Polish families from the neighborhood brought everything from their ripped dungarees to their torn slips for her to mend. She never would have understood why people wear ripped jeans today.

But more than just mending clothes, Babci became known for her skill at making old, worn clothing appear beautiful again. She was soon in high demand, particularly by the more well-to-do wives in town who wanted their old-fashioned dresses turned into the more modern looks.

Within a few years, her family went from living in a tiny house with dirt floors to a much larger house with cement floors, indoor plumbing, and a claw-foot tub, in a nicer town about 10 miles away. Babci remarried but soon got divorced, something that wasn't heard of in her day. She raised those four kids on her own, funded by her "sewing start-up." I think any venture capitalist today would be thrilled to invest in someone with talent and a work ethic like hers.

As poor as she was for most of her life, Babci taught us many lessons about how to live well. There were two in particular that she constantly reinforced. I have never forgotten them.

The first was wise advice about breaking bread with others. *When you have only one slice of bread and ten people come to your home, you butter it with the best butter and cut it into ten pieces. No matter what!*

When the milkman came to pick up his payment for the week on Saturday mornings, my Babci put her wisdom into action. She would buy challah bread and smoked fish every Friday night for dinner. But she always saved some for the milkman the next morning. And every Saturday, the milkman sat down with Babci and her family to share their little bit of bread.

The second lesson I learned the hard way. I was once helping Babci clean up the kitchen when I was seven years old and she caught me sweeping dust under a carpet. She grabbed my arm, spun me around, and with a stern, yet knowing look said, "Maria, never sweep things under the rug. It makes it harder to clean later."

While Babci wasn't out campaigning with the International Ladies' Garment Workers' Union for equal pay, she *was* a role model for my mother. She taught her that women could be strong and compassionate. And she taught her that women could not only take care of their families, they could take care of business, too. She was the first feminist I ever knew.

But to me, my mom is the ultimate feminist.

Mom thinks it was because she was raised mostly with my Babci and a clan of Bernardine nuns. My mom loved the nuns at St. Mary's, her school. She didn't see the nuns as subservient to the priests or the monsignor. She saw them as strong women who had made the choice to serve God. She knew the very moment that she met those nuns in grade school that she was supposed to serve God, too. She was like the heroine of *The Song of Bernadette,* the popular Hollywood film about the girl who saw the Virgin Mary in Lourdes, France. She decided she, too, would take the black veil with white trim, a long black dress, and "sensible" black shoes. She would become a bride of Christ.

Then she met Joe Bello. He was a year ahead of her in school, and the rest is history. When he ran away to join the army at 17, my mom concentrated on her studies. Most women of her generation didn't focus on their schoolwork because they weren't expected to go to college. Mom was different. She studied hard and became the only girl in her school to qualify for the National Honor Society. But Father Paul, the priest in charge of her high school, denied her admission. She learned that it was because of my dad. Apparently, Dad had done something really awful to piss off that priest. Sister Bernadette, Mom's 11th grade teacher, was outraged when she heard. She went to the priest to fight his irrational decision. Sister Bernadette couldn't understand how the priest could deny Mom her rightful place in the Honor Society just because of who her boyfriend was. It was as though Father Paul did not see my mother as her own person. Instead, she was just Joe's girlfriend. In the end, Father Paul won, but my mother never forgot the courageous nun who bravely fought for her. After high school, Mom had her "choice" of one of three professions acceptable to women of her generation: nurse, teacher, or secretary. Mom chose nurse, though she really wanted to be a doctor. She filled out her own applications and figured out how to apply to nursing school. Neither of her parents had graduated from high school, and they had no idea how to do such things.

She became a nurse at the Norristown, Pennsylvania, hospital where I was born a few years later. She was an ER nurse. (She was very helpful to me during my time on *ER*.)

By all accounts, she was a saint. She would never say this about herself, but in truth, given all she experienced in that hospital, she comes as close to a saint as anyone you'll ever meet.

There are a few experiences from her time in the ER that she will never forget. They shaped her worldview and pushed her to understand that she was indeed a feminist. There were many women who came in after botched abortions. They were too poor to pay a doctor to perform the then illegal operation. They either swallowed bleach or used knitting needles to end their pregnancies. Some had been raped. Others were too young to become parents. And many were forbidden to use birth control for religious reasons, had become pregnant with their seventh or eighth child, and simply could not afford another mouth to feed.

There was very little the doctors and nurses could do for these women. Many would leave the hospital never able to have children, and still others died from complications and infection. Though my mother was (and still is) a devout Catholic, and according to her faith women are not supposed to have abortions, Mom knew reality. Women would have abortions no matter what and they needed to have them safely. It was the poor women who suffered most. These women needed the power to choose what to do with their bodies.

My siblings and I, because we were raised in a household where our mother supported us with the help of my dad's disability pension, never considered that women were not equal to men. My mother never told my sister and me that we couldn't do something because we were women. She supported our decisions whatever they were. She raised two boys who are also feminists. My siblings and I have all raised our children to think the same way.

I've been dying to get my mom and Gloria Steinem together. I know they would love each other. They are on the same happy train. As Gloria says, "I've recently learned that laughter is the only free emotion." Mom certainly lives by this rule.

I'VE DECIDED THAT EVERY TWO AND A HALF MINUTES A NEW FEM-inist is born somewhere in the world. Okay, while I can't attribute this to a study by the Clinton Global Initiative or even *Ms.* maga-zine, my woman's intuition and my personal experience tell me it has to be true.

But really, what else would explain the growing global fem-inist movement around the common needs, aspirations, and desires of so many women from vastly different cultures?

That budding feminist could be a boy or a girl. He or she could be born in New York or Sudan. And yet many of these children could grow up not knowing they are feminists until some defin-ing moment brings them face-to-face with that label.

I've been lucky enough to travel around the world meeting women from countries and cultures vastly different from my own: Bosnia, Haiti, Kenya, Nicaragua, and many others. I always make it a point to see what we have in common. I've rarely met a woman who doesn't believe that she doesn't deserve social, political, and economic equality. And while we often start with very serious topics, usually we end up laughing about the stuff of everyday life. Some women proudly identify themselves as feminists. Some don't know they are feminists. But all of them support their families in some way: by working in fields, carrying their babies on their backs for 14 hours a day, or creating a safe space for their children and husbands in very challenging circumstances.

On one of my trips to Kenya, with Jackson and five of my female friends, I sat in a hut with seven Masai women dressed in traditional garb. The mother of a friend of ours had married a Masai warrior and had arranged for us to meet these women. They all had earlobes down to their shoulders, and shaved heads. We were wary of each other at first, asking only serious questions of each other about our daily lives. "Are you allowed to work?" "Do you have a say in your household and community?" "Are you paid the same as a man for the same work?" "Have you ever been physically or sexually abused?"

After sharing our more serious similar experiences, many of us were in tears. Then we became a giggling coven, talking about . . . what else? Sex. The Masai women even passed around a rolled-up napkin to show their preferred size of man. We traded more secrets as the conversation wore on. They said that in their culture, they each had a lover *and* a husband. They were shocked and saddened to hear that only one of us was married, until we explained that in our culture we were able to have many lovers, and it's called dating. The Masai women never did catch on to that concept, which is understandable since many of us in Western cultures have a hard time figuring it out and we've been dating for a long time.

In Bosnia at a refugee camp, I spent time with women who had seen horrific things during the war. In one moment, we were sharing experiences of violence and loss of husbands and lovers. And in another, we were sharing small acts of kindness, such as giving each other manicures and pedicures in our makeshift barracks. Women find ways to bond no matter what our circumstances. The more we know each other, the more we can support each other in standing up for our rights.

Feminism is a global movement defined and fueled by these common connections: our children, our faith in deep compassion, and our desire for equal opportunities economically, socially, and politically. I saw this everywhere I traveled and I felt it with every woman I talked to.

And it's through technology that we are discovering our common connections at an ever-increasing pace. Technology enables people, particularly women, who may never meet face-to-face, to share the surprising common threads of their lives—their struggles, their joys, and their hopes and dreams. Technology helps rapidly spread the reality that women are no longer victims, that women are becoming full participants in global policy. My organization, We Advance, helps women to connect all over Haiti. Soon perhaps women all over the world will have the same opportunity.

Twenty-seven years ago, when I was studying peace and justice education and women's rights at Villanova and working at the women's law project in Philadelphia, I read a passage that defines feminism in a way that is relevant to our lives today. It is from one of my favorite books, *Out of Africa*.

Karen Blixen, the author we know as Isak Dinesen and who was so beautifully portrayed in the film adaptation by Meryl Streep, had raised an orphaned bushbuck. She named her Lulu. Karen bottle-fed her, and for years Lulu roamed around her home as if she were Karen's own child. But as Lulu turned into a teenager, she disrupted the household tremendously: acting up, breaking furniture, and constantly trying to leave that secure place where she had always lived. And then one day Lulu disappeared. Karen was devastated.

Years later, Karen was doing the dishes at the kitchen sink

and when she looked out of the window, she saw a magnificent creature standing before her at the edge of the woods. She knew instantly that it was Lulu. She wrote, "Lulu of the woods was a superior independent being. A change of heart had come upon her. She was in possession. She was now the complete Lulu, the spirit of offensive had gone from her. For whom and why should she attack? She was standing quietly in her own divine rights."

The truth is that right now about half of the world's population is on the precipice of standing in our own divine rights and saying to the world, "You do not have to include us. We are including ourselves. We are empowering ourselves. And whether you like it or not, because of our common connections, we will succeed in joining to make our world a better place for our children in the future. We are not asking to sit at your table. We are saying you'd be lucky to have us."

We may still be fighting for and fighting against, but women all over the world are finding a new power, a new sense of themselves. We are advancing. Look at Malala Yousafzai, who won the Nobel Peace Prize in 2014. She almost lost her life fighting to be educated. But instead of shrinking away, she stepped further into her power by inspiring others.

And I am not excluding all of the smart and compassionate men out there. I have a son who is an incredible human being.

When I told him that some girls in the world were not allowed to go to school and that women in America made less money than men for the same job, he couldn't believe it. Though gender roles exist and maybe always will, there is a new consciousness in this generation of kids, and not only in America. When a young woman in India was raped and killed on a bus, the population rallied. Men and women of many generations stood side by side to protest the violence against women in their country. Sociologist Michael Kimmel is a great example of a man whose life mission is to create gender equality. He is considered one of the top feminists in our country.

I believe the new feminism is not about gender. The new feminism is an energy. It is a principle that men and women both possess. It is a trait that is defined by gentleness, compassion, and the heart. We are stronger together than we are alone, and we are moving into an age where these values can and must take the lead in all of our decisions.

The new feminism isn't about fighting against or for something; it's about standing in your own divine right. That's the woman I choose to be.

11

AM I LGBT OR W?

When I first wrote that Modern Love column in the *New York Times*, blogs, magazines, and tabloids made a big deal of my supposed confession. The headlines were predictable: "Maria Bello Comes Out as Gay," "Reveals She's a Lesbian in *New York Times* Piece," and "Comes Out as Bisexual." But in reducing my story to those terms, they missed the point. As the writer Mary Elizabeth Williams wisely put it in her article "Maria Bello's Great 'Whatever' Coming Out" in the online magazine Salon, the "big deal," for people like me, "isn't the gender of the person they're happy with; it's the happiness itself." She agrees, along with many others who have written to me over the past year, that people can change their sexual preferences throughout a lifetime or in a minute. As she said, "Maybe it makes for less simplistic headlines, but it's a lot more accurate."

MY FIRST ORGASM HAPPENED WAY BEFORE I KNEW IT WAS CALLED an orgasm. It wasn't with a man or a woman but with a pillow. I just felt the sensation in my body and I liked it. So back then I didn't know if I was straight, lesbian, gay, bisexual, or transgender, or a "pillower." I am thinking maybe we should change the label to LGBTP?

Yes, let's add a P. But not for *pillow*. Let's add a P to honor a great Black, Gay, Transgender AIDS Activist. Her name was Marsha P. Johnson. When people asked her what the P stood for, she said it meant "Pay It No Mind." To me, she was proclaiming herself a whatever.

In July 1992 I was sitting on a cement wall overlooking the Hudson River with a sweet boy from Long Island that I had been dating for a year. We were looking at the water on a sunny day, just minutes from breaking up. I was very into my full moon Goddess circles and rituals at the time and the down-to-earth Catholic boy was freaked out by that. I had told him I was a witch the day before. He didn't think his mother would approve and was about to tell me good-bye when I pointed at something bobbing in the water. "What's that?" I asked. He said, "A log." I said, "No, it's not. I think it's a head." When I walked closer to the pier I could see it clearly. "It's a fucking head!" It was a head attached to a bloated, fish-bitten gray-colored corpse. I asked a passing biker to get the police. My boyfriend ran away spooked, as he was sure I had conjured it.

Turns out the floating body was none other than the magnificent, black American, gay, transgender AIDS activist Marsha P. Johnson.

Afterward, I saw her photo on every street corner around Christopher Street where I lived. I remembered seeing this always-smiling, flamboyant, beautiful woman, but I never had the fortune to meet her. Her friends and supporters came forward to say that she was not suicidal as the police had theorized, but the police refused to investigate. The poster campaign said she had been harassed and gay-bashed in the very same spot where she died. It wasn't until 2012 that the New York City Police Department reopened Marsha's case. They now think that most likely she was murdered. I am currently trying to find out where the case stands, and to find ways to honor her.

Marsha was a true revolutionary for gay rights and for human rights. Marsha was one of the transgender folks who led the 1969 Stonewall Riots, at the bar in the West Village that was a half a block from my apartment. Marsha was at the forefront of that fight, and the many that followed in New York City as the LGBT community fought for equal rights. She started an organization to bring food and clothes to the young trans women who were living on the docks and nearby Christopher Street. She used her voice and her tremendous stilettos to create a better world.

Marsha is one of the reasons I became part of the LGBT community long before I slept with a woman. She taught me even after she was gone that it's not about who you sleep with, it's about who you fight for and who you love.

Let's be honest. Not everyone who sleeps with someone from the same gender cares about the great LGBT struggle for equality. They'll wink and nod at you like "Ooh cool, you're sleeping with a woman."

After my article, a woman came up to me at a luncheon and said, "Welcome to the club." She was a well-known lesbian in the entertainment community. I had known her a bit over the years and found her sneaky, hard, and a bit mean. I wanted to say, "I don't want to be in *your* damn club, you're an asshole." The club the woman was talking about was just about sexuality. And then I saw a man across the room, apparently a straight man who plays a gay man on a television show, and I thought, "The LGBT club he belongs to is the one I want to be a part of." A club that includes anyone who believes in human rights and allows anyone, regardless of what they call themselves.

The club I want to belong to is full of revolutionaries, fighting for theirs and other people's rights to love who they love. But like any club, I won't like everyone in it. I won't be interested in being identified with them.

Clare has never been part of a club and maybe that's why I fell in love with her. She never knows how old people are and never identifies anyone as black, white, Asian, etc. Sometimes I think she doesn't even know an elephant from a giraffe, and I love her for this. And she has always been a revolutionary. From a young age she was a part of the underground in Zimbabwe, working to help both black and white folks fight for their rights to choose their own governments and their own identities. She thinks many of them were probably LGBT, but as I've said, she's not one to label much.

When I met Clare, I had been with men almost exclusively. I fell in love with Clare from the first moment I met her, but not in a sexual way.

Five years ago, I was standing in front of a beautiful half-Chinese woman with short black hair at a fancy art gallery in New York City. She ran an organization that I hoped would donate to our work at We Advance in Haiti. I liked her very much, so I said yes when she asked me to join her and her girlfriend for a drink later that night.

Her girlfriend turned out to be the beautiful, curious, blond, blue-eyed Zimbabwean, wearing a bowler hat, who would be in my life from that moment on.

As I was looking through my photos while I was recovering from the parasite, I saw so many of the two of us, beaming with real love and laughter. And when I finally reached that black-and-white photo booth shot from New Year's Eve, a hummingbird magically appeared. I took it as a sign.

When I next went back to New York, I decided to proclaim my love to her. After spending a whole day together walking the streets in SoHo, we sat in a little Italian restaurant. I didn't know what to say at first. She and the girlfriend had been in therapy and were breaking up. I certainly didn't want to hurt her girlfriend, but I needed to admit my truth. When I finally had the courage to speak, I got all teary-eyed.

"There's something I need to tell you," I said.

She was concerned, as she thought I was going to tell her that I was dying of cancer or had gotten accidentally pregnant.

I finally said to her between my tears, "I think I'm in love with you."

It was a long, painful transition, going from friends to lovers. The process was tough for us and our mutual friends. And here we are, years later, with Clare sleeping soundly inside of our bedroom as I write outside on our balcony.

Clare has always been a whatever, having relationships with men and women, sleeping with some and not with others. It just doesn't matter to her. But it mattered to me when I saw that photo and realized I could in fact love her. I hadn't pictured living my life with a woman until then.

Here's the thing I got: she's not a woman or a man—she's Clare.

My mother taught me not to pray for a certain way a relationship should go, but to pray for a relationship to be the best that it is meant to be.

I hope that in the near future saying that you are LGBT will be just like saying what you prefer for breakfast. Why should we care who is having sex with whom? Or who is attracted to whom?

When I first kissed a girl at 21, it wasn't because I wanted to have sex with her. I just thought it would be fascinating to kiss a beautiful woman with bright red lips in a bathroom. It was a secret, so very sexy. But was that sex? Was I officially bisexual when I kissed the girl? Or was I officially bisexual when I was turned on by seeing two women kissing in a movie? Does the fact that I have had sex mostly with men in my life and have mostly fantasized about men mean anything?

I've wondered whether a man who has been married for 40 years but kissed a boy once when he was 10 because he was curious and attracted is bisexual. If a woman has only had sex with men, but fantasizes about a woman to have an orgasm, is she bisexual? How often and how far do you have to go to consider yourself bisexual? And if you *have* had sex with a woman and enjoyed it, but years later are only having sex with men, can you call yourself gay?

When people ask how long Clare and I have been together, I don't know what to say. Was it from that day at the bar when she gave me her hat? Or years later when we kissed? Or when we first had great sex? Or when we shouted our love out to the world?

I knew that the gender of the person I loved didn't matter, it was the love itself that mattered.

There are no labels that can define my relationship with Clare. This relationship, like all relationships, constantly evolves. Call it destiny, God, or whatever. . . . Clare was meant to be in my life. We teach each other and push each other to grow every day—and though the form of our relationship changes, the love is always the same. By the way, when people say to us, "You are a perfect couple," we always correct them and say, "It's mostly perfect."

So many people in the LGBT community have sacrificed so much to change policy, hearts, and minds. The entire world has benefited from their sacrifices beyond LGBT rights. The community has fought, marched, shouted, laughed, cried—all to move policies and to show the world it shouldn't matter to anyone who you love or who you sleep with. That's the part of the LGBT community I respond to the most. The struggle to love whomever you want without being disenfranchised.

An extraordinary thing the LGBT community has done is take back labels that were used to demean and disempower, and turn them into proud badges. Queer, Gay, Dyke, Lesbian, and Transvestite. Pretty much the terms I knew growing up.

So here we are today, calling our community of revolutionaries Lesbian Gay Bisexual and Transgender. Will we have to add more initials to honor all the communities who are defining their own identities, such as asexual, gender-neutral, trans-bi, etc.? And why not? These are people who ought to have their own rights, too. We own the URL www.wlgbt.com so we can honor whatevers—as a chuckle and a tie-in to my book, but also to be respectful to whatever anyone wants to call themselves.

So I consider myself a W, a whatever, and I am lucky enough to have found another W to love. I also take the label of LGBT and whatever other letter you want to add. But I will especially take P. Or we can just get rid of all the letters and instead use the phrase "Pay It No Mind." Because it's no one's business anyway. Thank you, gorgeous Marsha P. Johnson.

12

AM I RESILIENT?

Why can some people withstand so much hardship and still continue to find joy and bring joy to others?

Recently, my mother received a call from her doctor at the University of Pennsylvania in Philadelphia. He told her that her cancer was back.

She's had a peaceful three years without chemo, radiation, and worry. She should be a wreck. She should be crying. But, instead, she's making pierogies, that Polish specialty full of the most evil and delicious carbs. And she's laughing. She's not in denial. She's as joyful as she always has been.

My mom makes me laugh often and hard. The bellyache type

of laugh that makes it hard to breathe. She laughs so hard she pees her pants. Mom has always had a lack of bladder control, especially when she laughs. You would think in these moments that she must be stoned or drunk. She has never smoked, rarely drinks, and has never done an illegal drug. When she had a double knee replacement 10 years ago she made the nurses stop giving her morphine on the first day after the operation. She said it made her sick. The nurses were in awe, as they rarely had anyone refuse the pain drugs, especially just one day after surgery. I had a dose of morphine last summer when I was in St. John's being treated for the intestinal parasite. And I can say that without it I would have shot myself in the head because of the pain.

But Mom didn't want the drugs. Instead she listened to meditations on her iPod every day and did affirmations to get herself well. "I am healthy," "I am vibrant," "I am joyful," she would say over and over again as she took her first steps the day after the operation. She was in excruciating pain. She drew power from these mantras, and from her inner strength.

My mom, Kathleen Antoinette Urban, was born in a kitchen. She and her parents lived in a small apartment above the Brown Derby, the bar that my grandparents owned. This was in a small steel town 20 minutes outside of Philly.

Her earliest memories were of Mary, the mother of Christ. When she was two years old, my mom fell down a 12-foot staircase in her house. She says that she saw Mary at that moment, gently holding her and guiding her down the stairs. My grandmother was spooked when she heard this, as she couldn't explain why her two-year-old had fallen down the stairs and remained unharmed. But my mother could explain it. Mary had kept her safe.

Mom slept on the pullout couch in the kitchen and as my grandmother explained, "She never complained." My grandfather was a happy drunk. Always singing and laughing after shots of cheap whiskey. My Gram was always yelling at him to stop. She paid so much attention to him, that none really went to my mom. Mom was on her own, but never bitter about it. My grandfather, PopPop, was what you would today consider a highly functional drunk. He drank from morning to night with his buddies from the steel mill. Often he would bring his brothers and a few guys upstairs after the bar closed to sit around the kitchen table and play the accordion and drink whiskey, smoke cigarettes and cigars, and play pinochle. This was the best time of my mom's day. She would get up from her couch bed in the kitchen and serve the men Cracker Barrel cheese cut into perfect slices, along with salami and Ritz Crackers. She didn't do this because PopPop told her to. She just loved the music, celebration, and joy of family. By the time she was seven years old, she was making more complicated dishes like scrambled eggs for all the adults hanging out and singing at 2 A.M. She loved it. Cooking and sharing food was her passion and joy and continues to be so today.

A WEEK BEFORE I GRADUATED FROM HIGH SCHOOL, NEAR THE TOP of my class, my mother was first diagnosed with inoperable cancer. My mother and father sat crying in the den with its dark paneled walls and brown carpet and called us in to tell us. My mom was told she had five months to live and that it was time to put her "affairs" in order. I was in final exams at the time at Archbishop Carroll High School. The day after I found out, I had a big math exam. I stared at the test on my desk and saw that I already knew many of the answers. But in the pages that were supposed to contain answers to equations, I began to write in my essay book to my teacher, Sister Ruth, how afraid I was about what was happening. When I got my test back two days later, Sister Ruth asked me to stay after class and she gave me a long hug and said all the nuns would pray for my mom and family. She gave me an A.

But my mother was not one to give up. When that doctor at Memorial Sloan Kettering Cancer Center told her to "sort out her affairs," she uncharacteristically replied, "Go fuck yourself!" That was literally the first time she had ever said that word.

She started chemotherapy right away. None of us could be with her because she was being treated in Philly and we were all working at our Sea Isle City pizzeria at the Jersey Shore, trying to keep it afloat. After treatments all week, she would drive the two hours to come to the shore and make sticky buns. At the end of the day she would flop on the couch in our TV room and vomit in a bucket as she recited her mantras: "I am healthy. I am vibrant. I am joyful."

One night I came home crying at 2 A.M. after a night of fighting with my then boyfriend. I was trying not to wake my dad, who was passed out drunk. Mom called in from the den: "Marie, what's wrong, hon? Come here." And I went into the den and saw her on one of those couches with her half-bald blond head hanging over a trash can. I sort of flung myself onto the floor, indicating to her that my life was officially over. "Mom, I went to the bar to surprise him at the end of his shift, and he wasn't there," I wailed. "The manager told me he went with that girl who I saw him flirting with."

She got off the couch and gave me a huge hug as I was lying on the carpet crying. "Ah, hon, whatever happens it was the way it was supposed to. You just gotta laugh." I was a bit pissed that she didn't see how "serious" my situation was. Didn't she know this was the end of my life???? Of course, it was hardly the end of my life, but it was hard to escape the fact that she was potentially facing the end of hers.

Now, years later, what I remember the most is the white embroidery on the chest of the Laura Ingalls nightgown she was wearing that night, stained with vomit. I remember the look on my mom's face reflecting back at me. "I love you. More than life. I don't even care if I live or die. All I want is for you to be happy." And I lay there in my 1980s high-rise white-washed jeans and permed hair and continued to cry. It's a shame I didn't learn her lesson of laughter back then.

I was a little less self-indulgent the next time she told me she was going to die. Her cancer had recurred and the doctors again told her she wasn't going to make it through the year. I was 25 and had moved to New York to become an actor. When she was feeling well enough, she would take the two-hour train ride to NYC to make sure I had enough food. She would bring me homemade meatballs and sauce, schlepping up the steep flights of stairs to my tiny apartment in the West Village. Often she would come to the French bakery where I worked. She loved having a croissant and mint tea while she waited for me to finish my shift.

I would go back to Philly every weekend to spend time with

her after she finished a round of chemo. I could always find time even in between my jobs as a dog walker, French bakery waitress, and housecleaner. We would lie in her bed and watch *Oprah*. Oprah became our inspiration. She spoke to our hearts, made us laugh, and counseled us to remember our spirits and recognize that we all have a divine destiny on this earth. She reminded us of what my mom always knew to be true: that we are beautiful souls, living in human bodies, and our only job is to be a channel of light and bring our gifts forth. She would give my mom strength in many trying times.

Oprah was having some sort of competition during that time where you submitted a story about someone who changed your life and who you considered a hero. I decided to enter my mom into the competition. In one of my journals under my bed I found the letter that I wrote:

> *Dear Oprah,*
>
> *My beautiful mother is a walking MIRACLE. Eight years ago she was diagnosed with terminal lymphoma. The doctors told her to give up and she only had five months to live. But after all these years, she is still vibrantly alive, working and taking care of her family; she is more alive than anyone I've ever met.*

My mother is truly an angel. Everyone I meet knows
about her. I tell them about her beautiful spirit and
her capacity for love that is not of this earth. She was
a nurse for 15 years and I met people on the street of the
town we lived in who said, "Your mother was there until
my brother's dying day. She's an angel." After working at
the hospital she got a job at the local vocational school
in the poor area of town and began to teach nursing.
She is now an administrator at the Vocational School
working hard to change the educational system so
that the poor kids in the neighborhood have as many
opportunities as the Catholic school kids across the
street.

Three years ago, she was voted teacher of the year in
Philly. We received mounds of letters from ex-students
all saying the same thing, "Mrs. Bello changed my
life. She showed me for the first time in my life I was
worth it."

When my mother began her second bout with
chemotherapy—as her cancer became active again
and spread to other parts of her body—her spirit was so
strong it was clear she was fighting it with every ounce
of her being.

My family hasn't been away together on a family vacation in 15 years. Her dream is to take all her children away—she loves beaches, food, and celebration.

How can I begin to express to you how incredible she is and how deserving of this honor? Maybe this says it all: Saturday I sat with her after her treatment. We talked and laughed though she was wracked with pain. I asked for what she wished for more than anything in the world. I expected her to say, "To live," instead she said, "I just want you kids to be happy, to have everything you ever dreamed of." How completely selfless, compassionate, loving, and kind she is. She's my hero.

Thank you for taking the time to read this, Oprah. I know you are busy but you would miss a great opportunity not having my amazing mom on your show.

Sincerely
Maria Bello

I never sent the letter. But in the spirit of Oprah, I made a promise that I would make my mom's dream come true.

That summer, I saved $1,500 to take Mom on her dream

vacation to Italy before she died. She had flown on a plane only two times before, once to Disney World in Orlando and once to Acapulco for her honeymoon. I accounted for how much money we would need to survive for two weeks staying in hostels and small hotels in Rome and Florence and Venice and Portofino.

I will always remember her laughing and smiling as we landed in Venice. It was as if she did not have cancer at all. We took one of the famous vaporetto water taxis from the Venice airport to San Marco. We were in heaven, except for one small detail—our cumbersome baggage. Instead of the backpack I traveled through Europe with on my own, my mom and I bought fancy suitcases that we loaded onto those silver luggage dollies. Remember when luggage didn't have wheels and you needed a luggage cart? Ours broke on the first night in Venice as we dragged them for an hour down dark cobblestone alleys looking for our hostel. We were sweating and exploding with laughter at the same time.

"Marie, this is Venice," Mom laughed. "I thought it was supposed to be all romantic." But even if some of her romantic notions of Venice were dispelled in that moment, she took it all in with wonder and laughter. My mom and I spent two weeks heaving our broken suitcases and laughing the whole way.

There would be another recurrence in 2012. After a year and a half of chemo, her cancer cells had settled down. But just today, driving to my son's soccer game she got the call from the doctor. Not only is it back, but it's back in places that it's never been. Her non-Hodgkin's lymphoma has spread to her chest and groin and under her arms and on her spine. When she hung up the phone, she didn't look shocked. "Oh well," she said, "just another little blip on the road. The cancer gets so mad when I knock it out, it comes back stronger, but I'll get rid of it, no problem." And then we went to my son's soccer game, me in shock and her cheering him on.

So mom has been dealing with this for 30 years now. She took care of my dad and continues to do so more than ever since his MS has gotten worse. She's at our side whenever we need her. She's not perfect and will say so for sure. She gets stressed and sometimes acts the martyr. But when I ask her if she would do her life differently if given the chance, she says absolutely not.

This last summer, my parents took 16 of *us* on a trip to Italy for their 50th wedding anniversary. We rode around in a big bus to our grandfather's village and then to my grandmother's. We ate piles of seafood at our cousin Mario's restaurant and lit candles to Mary in every church. But the best memory from the trip is when my parents renewed their wedding vows. We were above the clouds, on top of a mountain in my grandfather's village in a chapel from the 1600s that looked out over forests and villages.

All of our family and the villagers came to the mass that the priest said in Italian. My parents sat in the middle of the aisle, my mom on a chair, my dad in his wheelchair. They held hands and cried. At one point he turned to her and said, "Look at these kids. We did good." And my mother gave him a sweet kiss. Yes, they have done good. Very good.

Mom always says that it just takes a quarter of a turn to change your life. One phrase that someone utters, a passage you might read in a book, or deciding to stay with someone or not can change your destiny forever. The phrase that constantly keeps me going is something she always says: "Whatever happens in your life, good or bad, ya just gotta laugh!"

I hope I will follow her lesson more and more, especially as she goes through this next phase of her illness. She says my specialty during chemo is making her laugh. We joke about how if she's seriously out of it, I promise I will always pluck her chin hairs, and that I will make sure she has a good wig for the wake when she dies.

Is this resilience? Resilience is about bouncing back. But it is also about fighting your way back. The synonyms are *strong, tough,* and *hardy.* My mother taught me that resilience is not just about being tough. It's about finding joy whatever happens in life.

13

AM I A WRITER?

"Am I a writer?" I ask myself daily. "Writer" is the term I added to my Facebook page and Twitter account a year ago. The word comes right after, "actor," "activist," and "adventurer." It takes chutzpah, I know, to label yourself, especially with labels that are usually given to you. But there's a method to my madness.

Most people know me as an actor. After I finished college, I went to New York City with $300 and two trash bags filled with clothes, because I wanted desperately to own that label: ACTOR. Turns out I had to *earn* that label instead.

I studied for years with the most brilliant acting teacher in the city, Fred Kareman. Fred was five one with a white close-cropped beard and hair to match. He was always chewing on a deli take-out coffee straw. His class was almost impossible to get into. He taught out of a small studio that had old wooden seats, originally from Carnegie Hall, lining the walls.

When I went to meet him, I felt like I was walking into a church. This was his holy ground. He was the priest of acting. I felt at home right away. I told him my background. I had taken a year of acting at Villanova and acting classes at the Wilma Theater in Philadelphia for a few months. He just sat chewing on his coffee straw and barely glanced up. "So, why do you want to do this, kid?" he asked.

"Well, I want to become a great actor," I replied.

He paused and then said, "Is there anything else you could possibly do? If so, you should go do that."

I didn't understand. He then continued, "If every ounce of your being does want this, just know you may fail and be a miserable old actress who does community theater in Iowa and slings hash at some restaurant."

Wow! This was not what I had expected. I thought Fred would take one look at me, see my passion, and say, "Yes, you are the one! Yes, you are brilliant. Yes, take my class and you will be a star."

Instead of welcoming me to the fold, he was trying to talk me

out of it. I started to panic. "No," I said, mustering my compo-
sure. "I have decided that this is the only thing I want to do."

He glanced up from his desk, looking over the top of his
glasses, and spoke in a holy, hushed tone. "Are you sure?"

I felt like I was about to enter the nunnery and was taking my
final vows. I was scared, but I was resolute. So in as convincing a
tone as I could manage, I said, "Yes, I am sure."

"Okay," he sighed. "Be here Tuesday at eleven A.M. sharp!"

I worked hard and went to class a few times a week. When I
wasn't in class I was practicing with my classmates. When someone would ask Fred how to get an agent or how to become a better
actor, he uttered only one phrase: "Just do the work, kid."

One of the greatest lessons I learned from Fred is "To thine
own self be true." He reminded us all that we didn't have to
"become" a different person to be a great actor. We just needed to
find those real places in ourselves that connected with the character. We were taught never to pretend, but to be in the moment
of the scene. It was a philosophy much like Zen Buddhism. When
you're washing the dishes, even onstage, all you have to do is
WASH THE DISHES. Simple, right? It took a very long to time to
learn this lesson, and frankly, I am *still* learning that lesson in
my acting and in my life.

It took eight years until I could make my living acting. And soon, people started recognizing me for that. I was no longer the "girl who wants to be an actress" or a "struggling actor," I was now a *real* actor.

Years later I would receive my first big acting honor, the New York Film Critics Circle Award for Best Supporting Actress in a film. I wanted Fred to present it to me, but he was in the hospital having just had surgery. That day of the ceremony, I went to visit him. And as I thanked him and went on and on about the lessons he had taught me, he just rolled his eyes and said, "Keep doing the work, kid." And I'll continue to do the work for as long as I can.

WHY DID I LABEL MYSELF WITH THE WORD "ADVENTURER"? I THINK that all started when I decided to take a break from Villanova, where I had been majoring in women's studies, political science, and pre-law. I had saved money from my job at Sbarro's fast-food trattoria in the local mall and took off for Europe.

By the end of my first three months traveling, I had joined a wedding in Amsterdam, drank beer at Oktoberfest with six friends I had met that day, and got pummeled (really, it was a massage) by a huge man in a loincloth in a basement bathhouse in Turkey. I was engaged at the time to a very lovely man. I loved him very much, but I had to do my version of sowing my oats before we would get married, become lawyers, start our own little firm, and live in a nice Jersey suburb.

When I stepped off the plane three months later I was dressed in my fabulous blue hat from Paris and black palazzo pants from the flea market in Amsterdam. I looked into the eyes of my handsome, perfect fiancé, who was there to pick me up with flowers in his hands, and knew it was over. I couldn't go back to life in Philly as I had known it. I had gotten only a tiny taste of what was outside of Philly and I wanted more.

I decided then that I would never get married. I wouldn't become a lawyer or a Jersey housewife. I had learned in a few intense months that I was an adventurer. I needed to see and experience new things, and seek out places outside and inside myself that I had never been to before.

JUST A SHORT TIME AGO, I ADDED "ACTIVIST" TO MY SET OF SELF-imposed labels. Activism is part of everything I do. In almost every article I write or interview I give, it always comes out that I am passionate about gender equality and have rolled up my sleeves to work alongside some amazing people all over the world. "Humanitarian" is not a label I am comfortable with, as you read earlier. An activist is someone who campaigns for or is actively involved with a social cause.

People who consider themselves activists come to it in different ways. Mine started right around grade school—although I don't ever recall not wanting to do something when I felt something was wrong or needed change. My mother told me that when I was 10 years old, my neighbor Martha Laydon and I became concerned about the factory down the street, which poured out black dust onto surrounding cars. Families on the street would go to bed with clean cars and wake up to see them covered with this mysterious dust. Some said it was the reason 6 out of 10 households on our street had a member with a case of terminal cancer. Martha and I went to investigate with our notepads. After we had climbed down the muddy hill that led to the railroad tracks where the factory was located, a man in a white jumpsuit caught us sneaking around. "Hey, you kids, what are you doing here?"

Even back then, I had some acting skill, I guess. Or maybe I had read too many Nancy Drew books. I improvised, telling the man, "Uh, we're doing research on all of the cool places in our neighborhood and how things are made and we wanted to see if you could show us."

He was more than happy to bring the two cute girls into the dank, miserable factory. Martha and I dragged behind him, pointing to the odd things we were seeing. Hundreds of yellow drums seeping sludge were piled up to the ceiling at the sides of the building. Something that looked like cotton candy was everywhere. I remember the first time I saw this stuff. It was when my siblings and I were enlisted to help my dad insulate the garage attic. I jumped on the pile of the foamy stuff. Dad screamed at me to get off. It turns out that insulation was made of asbestos.

They never told us what they were burning in that factory while we were sleeping. After the tour, they gave us pieces of gum and we left. We wrote up a report of our detective work and took it immediately to Sister Michael at our school. She was alarmed that we had gone there unsupervised and had lied to get ourselves a tour. My mother was equally upset, but also intrigued. Of course she didn't want me to get into trouble, but she was just as curious as I was to find out what they were burning. Years later, we would find out the truth, but not until my mother and dozens of our neighbors came down with cancer or died from it. When I became an adult I was interested in perhaps bringing a civil suit against the company. But they were long gone and their records were not to be found.

NOW TO THE FINAL LABEL—AM I A "WRITER"? I ADDED THE WORD to my profile. So does that mean I am one now?

I've wondered most of my life about this question. My mother said I was born a writer. (Okay, so she's my mom and unconditionally loves me. But she's got a discerning eye, really!) At age seven, I was obsessed with writing in my pink Holly Hobbie diary. I would make up stories, accompanied by stick-figure people with speech balloons above their heads.

At age nine, I was reading every romance novel I could get my hands on. The one I remember most was by Kathleen Woodiwiss. The heroine, dressed up like a boy, stows away on a pirate ship. The captain catches her in the lie and they fall for each other and make tender love. She is confident—a swashbuckling crusader who fights like a man and has the values of a superhero. She and other similar characters inspired me to write my own love stories. By age 12, I had graduated to more serious-looking journals and notebooks—still covered with hearts and flowers—and was writing every day.

I still write almost every day. By now I've been writing for more than three decades.

However, for many years, I didn't get paid for my writing. And, based on that criterion, I didn't consider myself a writer. I realize now that I was actually a "struggling writer" but was too frightened to call myself that. Maybe it had to do with how terrifying it was being a "struggling actor."

The only struggle I had as a writer was figuring out how to get paid for it. Otherwise, I was a prolific writer. I wrote all the time. I wrote my version of the "Great American Novel." I wrote and directed a play. I wrote numerous screenplays and a television pilot. But I never sold anything. . . . So I guess I wasn't a writer. At least I didn't think so.

Finally, after more than 30 years of writing, I got paid. In November 2013 I got paid to write a piece for the *New York Times*'s Modern Love column. I also wrote a follow-up piece for them the next week, and got paid again! Then publishers approached me and asked me to write this book based on the themes introduced in the articles. Maybe now I'm a writer?

I won't deny it. Seeing my name in print in the *New York Times* and then writing this book were two of the best moments in my career. But the most gratifying moment came when Jackson finally read the first article, months after it was published. He saw the article framed on our bedroom wall—a gift from Clare. Jack texted me as I was sitting at my very dear friend Mariska's birthday celebration in Connecticut. I love that I was at Mariska's, since it was she who had introduced me to Jack's dad. I always say she is responsible for the birth of Jackson Blue McDermott.

Jack's text was astounding. It's too precious to share. When he writes his book, he'll decide if he wants to publish it. Basically, he said that the article had made him proud to be my son and part of our modern family. He knows how his words and his support inspired me to write that article in the first place. I credit him

185

with helping me begin to understand what it means to be truly happy. So back to this notion of whether I'm a writer.

My friend Claudia, who is a brilliant writer but great at everything, if I'm honest, recently told me that "An accountant can consider him or herself a poet. It's about what's in your soul, not what's on your W-2."

My friend Darcy also calls herself a writer. She pays her rent by being a nanny and tutor. She has been paid for her writing. She was a writer of erotic fiction under a nom de plume while living in Paris. When she has time, she writes screenplays and has studied writing for years. She is brilliant. But would you call her a writer if you knew she was also a nanny and tutor by day?

Clare makes her living being a creator of ideas, brands, and strategies. When people ask Clare what she does, she says, "Nothing." This always takes them off guard, as the word comes out of an obviously brilliant woman with great style and a cross between a British and a Zimbabwean accent. That is what brought her to the United States in the first place. At 22, she sold an animated movie to a big Hollywood studio and moved to LA. Her screenplay is about two twin rhinos that go on a hunt to save their mother. The movie was never made, but she was paid for writing it, so is she a writer? To her the answer is yes. In her soul, she considers herself a writer.

When I was 28 years old, traveling alone for the first time in Africa, I met a man at the Johannesburg airport. I was sitting writing in my journal, and became afraid when I heard screaming coming from the main terminal. This was during the Soweto uprising, so I worried there had been an attack on the airport. Later, I learned that it was a group of young students coming back from a choral competition. They and their parents were screaming and crying for joy at their victory.

But at the time, I didn't know this and I was afraid. While I was trying to stay cool and not panic, a kind-looking man came up to me and calmed me. Here's what I wrote after he walked away:

> A man, about 65 years old, approaches me as I sit and write. In a broken accent he asks if I am writing a book. I say, "Maybe one day." He says, "Remember that I asked you this always, about this book you will write." I will always remember the premonition of Mr. Rashita from Israel and hope one day he will read the book he sees me write.

Mr. Rashita, if you are reading this book, thank you very much!

Here's what I have decided. You are what you love doing. I love writing even when I don't like it or when I feel it doesn't like me back. I am learning to embrace this truth.

5-SUBJECT NOTEBOOK
200 SHEETS/WIDE RULED/10½x8

NATIONAL BLANK BOOK COMPANY, INC. • HOLYOKE, MA. 01040   37-064

EAGLE
LINE

14

AM I ENOUGH?

Do you sometimes have those moments of complete despair when no matter what good is happening in your life, you feel so alone and afraid?

I used to think of myself as a broken bird, trying to fly and bandaging my own wounds, but never able to get off the ground. Eventually, I decided that someone else could mend my wings and *then* I would magically take off. I have been on many spiritual quests that I hoped would fix me. Am I fixed? Was I actually broken?

When I moved to NYC at 21, spiritual seeking became my mission along with becoming an actor. I was sure that someone "godly" was going to tell me what was wrong with me and heal my wounds. The first year in the city I was as unemployed as any actor could be. I was waitressing and bartending, hoping to be discovered. I had decided that to become a great actress, I must go back to my past and rid myself of all the demons in my life. The demons were the things that made me such a lonely girl, kept me at a distance from people. I was afraid if other people got to know me, really know me, they would see how broken I was and feel sorry for me. Feeling sorry for me meant that they thought I was weak. That was my biggest fear. I knew what weakness could do to someone.

So I made friends with another actress who claimed to hold secret "Goddess" knowledge for healing. She told me she knew channelers and healers and psychics who could make me all better. The girl, Beverly, was a bit wacky at times and dramatic. She wore big white pirate shirts and black capes. She had raven black hair and big brown eyes, and really white skin. She was an ex-model and astoundingly beautiful. She seemed to have it all together. I wanted to be like her.

We struck up an unlikely friendship when I was invited to her apartment one night for a full moon Goddess circle. I showed up in my combat boots and ripped jeans; she was in some diaphanous white dress. She used an eagle feather to "cleanse" me and the three other girls with sage, put on some Enya, lit all the candles in the place, and began to conduct the circle. One after the other we were told to give up the baggage that was holding us back from our highest good and leave it in the circle. We had to say what we were giving up. I was pretty vague. "My pain. My past. My control." We danced around and sang a chant and then made a wish on the full moon. Beverly told us that it was ancient knowledge that anyone who made a wish on the full moon would get his or her wish fulfilled. (I think I wished that John F. Kennedy Jr. would fall in love with me.)

Then we ate some healthy food and drank red wine.

I felt amazing afterward. Better than I had for years. Now, I realized, my healing wasn't about going to a shrink and rehashing old events from my past. It was about just letting it all go, connecting with the spirit inside of me. Moving *above* the concerns of the world and moving *away* from my own negative concerns. I didn't need JFK Jr. anymore; I was my own beam of light.

What a breakthrough! For six months I dedicated myself to practicing my newfound spirituality. And only occasionally (10 times a day, as opposed to 100) fantasized about my dream man. I adhered to all the advice Beverly gave me so that I would become "cleared" and ready to move on to the "next phase of my existence." I stopped eating dairy and stopped smoking, because they "blocked the flow of information and made me an impure channel." I started to see a Rolfer who literally tried to dig the pain of my past out of my body. It hurt. A lot. I did Beverly's meditations. I went to her place for seminars. One time I went to meet a man who claimed to be an alien from a different universe. He made steel pyramid hats that you would wear on your head to contact extraterrestrial life. (Only the good kind, of course.) He was quiet and smiled like some idiot savant. I was only alarmed when he went into the bathroom and came out with a bar of pink soap in his hand. He looked curiously at the 10 of us gathered and asked, "What is this thing used for?"

For the next two decades I continuously pursued spiritual truths and psychological healing, and visited every doctor, healer, psychic, shaman, and channeler under the sun. I read every self-help, new age book under the sun. And I loved all of it. And I learned from all of it. And it made me more curious and helped me to get through some hard times. But at a certain point, I felt that I had done enough searching outside of myself, so I finally stopped looking. One day, some years ago, cleaning out my bookshelf, I saw that most of these books were saying the same thing. They were usually written by some "authority" attempting to teach you what you can only teach yourself. By telling me over and over again the answers were inside of me, I guess I started to listen.

So I surprised even myself when I ended up recently in the office of a newly famous celebrity doctor. As I had recently quit smoking, I was uncovering some deep feelings that had been hidden under the smoke. Smoking cigarettes has been my addiction for 30 years. I wanted someone to magically take it away. I was also stressed after doing six movies in a row and being away from home much of the year. My now teenage son and I had our biggest blowout and I was having "not-good-enough mommy" syndrome. I was running on empty, trying so hard to keep up with Jack's life, Clare's, my job, Haiti, and the book, I forgot to take care of myself. I was exhausted. I wanted desperately for someone to tell me how to do it, since I couldn't figure it out on my own.

The new doctor drew me in right away. He looked so happy and tranquil in his photos and he had rave reviews from celebrities that I admire.

Before seeing him, I had to fill out 20 pages of paperwork. The first question was, "Why do you need to see the doctor?" In my second-day detox haze, I wrote: "I need urgent care for a lifestyle change. The lifestyle I've been living has me running on empty, feeling stressed, smoking, and is causing me physical, emotional, and spiritual pain." (Sounds like me at 21, right?) And the second question was, "Why would you like to see the doctor?" What I should have written was, "Many Hollywood people, especially an actress I really like, keep saying how you changed their lives. And today I want to change mine." Instead, I was vulnerable to a man I did not even know so I wrote: "I heard so many wonderful things about you and had a sign yesterday to contact you. I woke in the morning and knew I could not continue my life as I have been living it."

Within a day he called me and left a voicemail. His voice sounded soothing and kind. He ended with "I am at your service and send you love." I was thrilled that a guy who had a year's waiting list, even with celebrities, was going to see me within a few days!

He was ridiculously expensive, especially on "off hours." He said he never came in on Wednesdays, but he said he knew he was supposed to for me. He came in on Wednesdays *only* for cancer patients.

I got very lost going to his healing center in the middle of nowhere outside of LA, so I was quite stressed when I arrived. I was out of the cigarette detox phase by now, and feeling pretty good from resting, not smoking, and being kind to myself and making up with Jackson. I worried that I didn't have anything to talk to this healer about. Still, I felt special when the good-looking doctor came into the small room where a nurse was taking my vital signs, and I stood up and gave him a hug. "I feel like I know you," I said. Because that is what you say to new age folks that you don't really know. He said the same and looked deep into my eyes.

When I was escorted to his office, he looked different, now

in his white lab coat and serious expression. There was a Virgin Mary in the corner of his room. "Wow," I said. "Mary, I love Mary. My mother has had visions of her since she was a little girl, and every time she is in a bad health situation, she smells roses or is given a rose or finds one by surprise and knows Mary is looking after her." He gave me a questioning look. I suppose not many of his patients said such things.

He sat across from me and looked in my eyes and took a breath. "Just know whatever you say stays in this room. I will never share what you say with anyone." My ears perked up. I learned a long time ago that if someone you've just met tells you that, you have to beware. Usually it means they will tell someone. Thank God I didn't make the same promise.

He began with, "How can I be of service? What do you need?"

I immediately got right to the point, "I have done many modalities of healing. I was very sick last summer so I know I am healthy now, as I've had many tests as you can see on my blood test chart. I meditate, do yoga a bit in the morning, see an acupuncturist, and get vitamin therapy and take supplements." Turned out that his big sell is selling all of those things but for 10 times the average price.

"So what do you need?" he said.

I said I had read in his magazine about a new psychosocial

program that was integrative. I said I felt that my smoking blocked me somehow and I wanted to open up more emotionally and spiritually. Now this is no new age information. Smoking pushes down emotions and takes time away from family, so you feel disconnected, at least I do. I was using it to dull the pain of being menopausal and middle-aged and not finding a new dream to chase. I went on to say that I'd seen many different kinds of healers and told him what one of my mentors had told me: "You dare people to like you." I told him that I knew he couldn't fix me, that the answers were all inside me and I just needed to love and accept myself. I cried a bit talking about needing a new dream and trying something different and about some regrets I had. He looked at me with a stern look and then came over to the couch and kissed me on the head.

I thought it was a little strange, but like I said, I've been to many of these kinds of folks and they do similar things. The doctor said, "You don't love yourself."

"Well, certainly not this last week," I said, laughing. I had been a bitch with Clare and short with Jack, so I definitely wasn't feeling much love.

I told him that I was in a romantic relationship with my best friend, Clare, after being with men most of my life and he seemed shocked. I told him he should read my article from the *New York Times* and that I was writing a book inspired by it. He then exploded. He looked at me like a madman and said, "What book? You have nothing to write! You can't write a book! What are you going to talk about? You don't even know or love yourself!" I tried to tell him what the book was about. He then said, "Oh, I got you, they don't know, they don't know, I see what you do. . . ." He really looked like a madman now and popped off his chair and said, "You've walked around your whole life with a big dildo pointed at everyone, telling every man to fuck off. You need to open your pussy! You cannot receive; you need to receive a man."

Seriously, that's what he said. And I didn't leave. I started to believe once again that this man knew much more than I did about me. I listened. He sat back down and drew out a graph for me with odd words he had invented but that made no sense. As he scribbled down the page explaining, I said, "I'm usually pretty smart, but can you explain again, because I have no idea what you are talking about." He looked at me. I don't think he was used to people asking him questions.

Then he looked at me and wrote a word, "sychotic," and a line going up a graph like up a huge hill. "This is you," he said.

"I'm psychotic? Did you spell it wrong?" I asked. "I don't think I am. I haven't gone off my meds or anything and . . ."

He stopped me. "Most people are here." And he pointed to another graph—this one with a straight line and then tiny little anthills popping up. "These are normal people and this is you."

He pointed to the "sychotic" line. My line was *way* off from the normal. I stared at him and he flew across the room to his desk and pulled out a Bible.

He rolled back and opened a page dramatically where he had underlined "The meek shall inherit the earth." I knew the phrase well after 16 years of Catholic church and since my mentor was a Catholic priest and all.

He asked if I knew what it meant. I said, "Humility." I had prayed since I was sick last summer for grace and humility, to help me be open to whatever it was God wanted me to do.

He raised his voice. "And do you know what humility means?"

"Um," I said, "to be on your knees and know you don't know everything and God will take care of it. And no human will fill God's place?"

He then said, "Do you know where the word HUMILITY comes from?" I was stumped and wanted to call Jackson, as he has been taking Latin for two years. And the doctor blurted out, "HUM-MUS!" The dip? I thought. "Hummus means soil. You have to be in the soil to be meek." I felt relieved. I'd certainly felt dirty all week, detoxing.

It seemed he finally got tired of explaining and of me saying, "Oh, I get it so . . ." And he pulled out a book and rolled back over again, nodding his head and looking at me suspiciously. It was a book of faces. A teen with acne, a woman with wrinkles, a man with a lopsided face. "*This* is what's wrong with you!" he said.

"Something's wrong with my face?" I asked.

He said, "When I came into the office and surprised you, that's part of my analysis. I like to catch people off guard to see how they really are and read their face." I thought about his hug and wondered how I had measured up. Thank God I didn't just shake his hand and lower my eyes; he would have thought I was really psychotic.

Time was almost up so I asked, "So what do you think I need?" I was serious. I thought he would tell me that I needed deep psychotherapy with him. But he wrote the name of another doctor down on a paper.

"This is my teacher who taught me cranial sacral. You need to get your face and mouth straightened out first. Your forehead and cheeks are not open enough and the right side of your face droops and your mouth is too tight, your teeth are too crowded."

I didn't take any offense, as I knew my teeth were a bit crowded and the right side of my face slightly drooped. But only slightly. It's not like magazines published photos of me with headlines like LOOK AT HER DROOPY FACE!

He then said, "You can spend twenty-five thousand dollars with me in my special celebrity and powerful people one-on-one therapy sessions but first you have to get this situated." I was in a bit of a daze at this point. I came here for the guy to say, "You are too fucked up for me to help you"? He hugged me good-bye, looked deeply into my eyes, gave me his cell phone number, and said again, "I am at your service, whatever you need."

After signing a copy of his new book for me—about how to lose weight—I thought, "Well, at least I don't need that." And we walked into the lobby. I caught the eyes of another woman who was sitting there with a cute young man. I realized she was a celebrity whom I knew. We gave each other hugs and hellos. The doctor took the young man into his office, looking a bit annoyed. I guess he didn't just see me and cancer patients on Wednesdays, but beautiful celebrities and their young boyfriends as well.

After I paid my $600—and I almost threw up signing that receipt (I could have given that money to my sister to spend on her Italy trip or even to be nice to myself and buy a few pairs of shoes)—I thought about what he had said. "He really helped me," I thought. And that's what I told Clare when I got home. I believed it. Clare wasn't having any of it. She listened to me, with all the earnestness in my voice. And then she looked at me like I was *really* psychotic.

She pulled up his book from the side of the bed and started reading me the quotes that appeared in the front pages, all written by celebrities. "Dr. Heal Me is the most compassionate, kind person." "He changed my life with his gentleness and guidance." On and on they went. I was slightly devastated but laughing at the same time as she read on. He definitely wasn't very gentle or kind to me. Clare and I talked about how we all look for someone outside of us at times to tell us who we are and to make us feel better. When people you respect tell you that a particular person has the answer to make you happy, we often believe them. I find often with folks who preach that they have an answer to your existential pain, it's mostly what you know already—the answers are in yourself and your relationship to your higher power. This doctor was the same kind of healer I met when I was 21, trying to tell me what was wrong with me. "Same guy, different name," I like to say.

I thought back to all of my spiritual seeking. I didn't have *the* answer, but I thought I had *some* answers then. I thought that I could bypass my pain by going directly to the spirit. All the rituals I did made me feel good in the moment, but they ended up being temporary bandages. When they fell off, I was still bleeding. I remembered all of the things the well-meaning Beverly told me. If I do this meditation once a day for 40 days, I will no longer be depressed. If I light this candle for seven days, my soul mate will appear. If I, if I, if I . . .

I think now that life doesn't really work like that. For years

I went to channelers, healers, psychics, and astrologers. I met a reincarnated Christ and three reincarnated Buddhas. I have done sweat lodges and vision quests, done yoga, and lived by tarot cards. I have explored every church, every theology, philosophy, and ideology. And I saw that quack doctor. They all helped me, for a while. Some for only a few minutes. But in the end, none of them could really fix what was broken inside of me or give me something that I never had. All I wanted was to be okay. To be a better, stronger person. To make the demons go away. They never do, but they do get quieter as I get to know myself more.

So I don't believe anymore when someone tells me that they have THE ANSWER. These are the people you should run away from, quickly. I think they wouldn't be human if they had the answer. I've met people who are supposed to be the holiest, wisest people in the world who have turned out to be very unkind. I have met a limousine driver who seemed to have more answers and clarity of vision than any "healer" I have ever met. Life is just complicated that way. And interesting. Go figure.

And yet there are other spiritual teachers who have given me pieces of advice that I will never forget. Most I've never met and probably never will, but their words inspire me still. One of the first was Florence Scovel Shinn, who was born in 1871 and wrote the book *The Game of Life and How to Play It*. She spawned the idea of visualization and positive thinking and putting love above all else. Those who came after her—Marianne Williamson, Melody Beattie, Paulo Coelho, Tony Robbins, Shakti Gawain, Deepak Chopra, Eckhart Tolle, and many more—all helped me to love myself a little more. But Dr. Heal Me certainly didn't!

Seems to me in my journeys that the people who tell you they have *the* answer are the ones you should simply avoid. But I know that *no* human can relieve our craziness and our humanness. I went to that quack doctor saying, "There's something wrong with me." So of course he agreed!

The day after I saw him, I woke up in a shitty mood realizing that I had just spent $600 to get the same answer once again. I knew I had to look within myself for the answer, but I couldn't remember how to do that and I didn't have the energy. It's like being on a diet. You know what to eat; you just have to make your-self do it. All the books and doctors say the same thing, just in different packages. You are the only one who can actually *not* put that Cheeto in your mouth.

So in my sulking, bitchy, negative state, I went to sit on the sand overlooking the ocean next to our home. I closed my eyes and started to breathe. With every exhale I saw my dark thoughts, which I call my shadow self. With every inhale, I tried to see my inner light and joy.

I prayed.

My mother told me not to pray for the release of my pain, but to ask to be filled up with peace, love, and joy. So I asked that of God.

Please enter me and fill me with your grace. Help me to see my value and worth. I have everything. I ask you dear God with all my heart to heal me in this moment. Show me the way to you. Help me believe in myself. I cannot save myself. I need you to give me meaning and some relief. You seem so far away right now.

I realize what I've always been looking for was a closer connection to God. I wanted to have a gentle relationship with both my light and shadow self and accept myself fully. I needed to trust that my connection to God would always lead me back to the light.

So I asked God, *Where are you?*

Suddenly I heard a voice deep within me.

Asking questions is good. It means you are open to growing, changing, and becoming who you were always meant to be.

I'm right here, partner. I've never left.

EPILOGUE

I hope this book is the beginning of a lifelong conversation for me, and for everyone who reads it. I hope we all keep questioning the labels we give ourselves and others, regarding relationships, family, race, religion, sexuality, age, weight, height, culture, mental and physical abilities, and basically, everything else under the sun.

I wrote this book as a series of questions, because at the start of every journey is a question. Part of the word *question* itself is *quest,* and each of these questions carried me along as I examined myself, my world view, and where I fit. Some of the answers I came to were surprising. Other answers were more expected. But the exercise of examining what I thought about these topics and these labels pushed me to more fully embrace the woman I have become. We are all constantly "becoming." That is one of the joys of life. Nothing is static. My ideas in this book aren't static—as the years go by my opinions will certainly change, colored by age and experience. The relationships I've written about will continue to evolve. Some will grow stronger. Some will fall apart. The only certainty is that in a few years, they will all be different from what they are now.

Even in the course of writing and finishing the book, situations arose that surprised me and made me realize just how fluid things really are.

The person I was most terrified of reading the book was the first one to read it—my Pop. I didn't want Pop to be hurt and angry because of my frank disclosures about his behavior during our childhood. He was visiting me in California when I finished writing. Without my knowledge, he took a copy and read the whole book in one sitting. He thought the stuff about him was right on, but had a pretty hard time with the chapters that included "the sex stuff," as he called it. Exactly what you'd expect from a dad, I guess. But all of the fear I had felt putting our story out into the world melted away—my dad's acceptance of how I wrote our story shows just how our relationship has healed.

Speaking of "Fathers"—after months of looking for a Catholic parish to accept us so that Jack could apply to his Catholic high school, we found one who did so with open arms. The monsignor welcomed us immediately with the statement "I read your article, and it's so wonderful! Jackson sounds like a very soulful and insightful young boy." I was so thankful. This is the Catholicism that I know. The one that Father Ray showed me.

My mother proved not to be the complete saint I painted in these pages. Soon after the book was finished, she told me to park in a handicap space as we were very late for church. We had Pop's handicap sign in the car, but something still didn't feel right to me. "Mom," I said, "we can't park here. Can you at least limp?"

In her hilarious way, Mom replied, "You know I'm a terrible actress. I'll tell them I have cancer! Just because I'm not balding doesn't mean I don't have cancer. What are they gonna do, throw me out?!" Mom was willing to push the rules—she's earned the right after all. Mom does still have cancer, and in the next months we'll all be locking arms around her to fight that demon once again. But we'll all keep laughing.

I also recently went back to Haiti, but this time not in the guise of a humanitarian. I went to see my friends Lolo and Caro and my extended family. I went to the beach I missed so much. I saw a country that I wouldn't have recognized two years ago. Its roads are clean and the tents are gone. Haiti isn't healed yet, but she's on her way. I can't wait to see her again, this time with even more hope for the future.

And I was inspired by something my son said recently about feminism without even knowing or using the word. When I told him he had to take an academic course for his free period instead of Ping-Pong, he was placed in gender studies. He looked at me with surprise and said, "Gender studies, what's that about? Why do we even need it? Everyone already knows girls and boys are equal." I was so proud of him. I was also excited for him to learn about the incredible courage of the women and men who have fought for these ideals. I want him to learn that the kind of equality he sees is coming, but we aren't there yet.

And I realized that my visit to Dr. Heal Me wasn't all bad. At the time that I saw him, I was running out of time and energy while writing this book. He threw me my Hail Mary. He gave me the material for the last chapter *and* a good laugh at myself for paying someone once again for me to realize that I didn't need fixing because nothing was broken. I am already whole—just complicated, wounded, loving, difficult, and kind. I have finally discovered the joy that comes from hitting bottom and pushing oneself up to the top again.

My journey has been a series of hits and misses, miseries and

obsessions, spiritual seeking and love. It has been about finding
myself and finding self-acceptance. This is my wish for you.

IT IS NOW JUST BEFORE THIS BOOK IS TO BE PUBLISHED. I AM SIT-
ting at the slate white-and-gray kitchen island of our rental
house. What I see is a kitchen I've always dreamed of—open to the
dining room and living room, filled with light coming in from
the floor-to-ceiling glass doors. There are beautiful photos on
the walls. Many are from my travels around the globe, from Mas-
sachusetts to Morocco. But the ones I love best make me smile
and break my heart at the same time. They are the ones of my
family. These photos capture a moment in time that will never
exist again and a family that will always be changing. When I
look at other pieces of art in the house, like the steel mesh skele-
ton of a woman's dress that the real owner of the house created, I
remember this isn't really our house. We are renting this space.
And I see in a way that we are renting the relationships with the
people we love as well. We do not own them. As I do not own this
house. We pay money for renting homes and cars. But what we
pay for loving is much more expensive. We sometimes pay for
loving with heartbreak, challenges, loss, sadness, and pain.

In this book I have shared my views on the beauty of the fluidity of love and partnership. And it *is* beautiful. But sometimes,

it just plain *sucks.* As with all transitions, we are forced to shift even though we may not be ready. Each individual in a relationship has his or her own story, needs, wants, and desires. When those are in conflict with our own, sometimes we can reconcile, but other times, the universe has a different plan. I do know, deep in my heart, that if I just give all of my relationships up to my partner, God, everything will be better than I could have ever imagined.

Life is changing quickly. Every day the conventional view of family and partnership changes. It's challenging for some to grasp the new words and labels that are evolving. But it is also a lot more exciting, if you ask me. We are expanding our lexicon to include families of all stripes, relationships that defy description, and unconventional partnerships. The old ideas of love, marriage, children, and happily ever after just don't apply to most of us. I have come to see that the labels that other people might give me about my partnerships, family, ethnicity, sexuality, religion, and spirituality do not define me. I am only concerned with the only labels that matter—the ones I give myself.

Let's continue to ask questions to figure out who we are, who we want to be, who we love, and who we want to share our lives with. Labels are useless and meaningless, unless they are the labels you want for yourself and make you feel part of a community to which you are proud to belong. Labels should never make you feel judged or afraid.

Finally, truth is, call me whatever you want! I will label myself practically anything to advance human rights. All I hope is that we all keep questioning our labels, get rid of the ones that hold us back, and hang on to the ones that shine light on the beauty of who we really are.

SENDING GOLDEN SHOES TO YOU AND ALL WHOM YOU LOVE.

Maria

ACKNOWLEDGMENTS

When I was 21, a woman in a casting office asked me what I wanted to do with my life. I said, "I want to change the world." Grand ambitions for such a young girl! Later in life I realized that for me, it was the little things that I could give that would help change the world. We all have gifts to offer and this book is one of mine.

There are many people who have supported me in giving my little gift. To my team at HarperCollins and Dey Street Books—my publisher, Lynn Grady; Jeanne Reina; Paula Szafranski; Joseph Papa; Sharyn Rosenblum; Michael Barrs; and Sean Newcott— thank you for helping me to continue the conversation of labels.

I'd especially like to thank my editor, the brilliant Carrie Thornton, who trusted me and allowed me the space to find my voice while always making what I had to say even better. But mostly though, by being yourself—a perfectly imperfect working mom. You made me feel not so lonely anymore and gave me the confidence to keep going.

John Carrabino, Heidi Schaeffer, Bob Myman, Kim Hodgert, Rick Kurtzman, Michael Rosenfeld, Marie Ambrosino, Michael Katcher, Cait Hoyt, and Alasdair Munn, you have been my guides to a career I've always dreamt of. Whether I've been up or down, hot or not, you believed in me and are honorable, trusted colleagues, and most importantly, friends.

Thank you to my friends and family for letting me tell their stories and for their constant support: Mom, you are the sunshine for all of us. Pop, Joey, Lynn, my best friend and sister Lisa, Dave, my savior bro Chris, Brittany, Maya, Kylie, Tyler, Christian, Carly, Sophia, Aunt Connie and Uncle Pete, Aunt Sheila and Uncle Pat, Uncle Ed, my Grandma Fran, Uncle Denis and Aunt Roe, and all my cousins. Also the ones who are not here with us: PopPop Urban, Grandma Bello, PopPop Bello, Babci, Aunt Gert, Uncle Stosh, Aunt Margaret, and my Aunt Maria, who all helped to make the Farkel family what it is today. They help us all to keep laughing and to continue to make lemonade out of lemons!

My friends for life—Kelly Loftus, for your grace and humor and for always loving me, and Carolyn Mayer, who made me feel cool even in high school. Camryn Manheim—I am so lucky our boys are brothers. You've helped me to become a better mom. Aimee Carpenter and Leslee and Laura Feldman—my sisters who first showed me the beauty of an untraditional family. Ray Azoulay, who always has my back and makes me smile and who gave me the old typewriter when I signed the deal for the book with a note that said, "Start writing right away."

To Kathy Eldon, Suzanne Lerner, Gretchen Thomas, Lolo Silvera, Caroline Sada, Barbara Guillaume, Aleda Fishman, Alison Thompson, Captain, Danielle Saint-Lot, Bryn Mosser, Beth O'Donnel, Karim Amir, Jehane Noujaim, Christina Lurie, Dick Friedman, Sue Munn, Josie and Alan Munn, Paul Haggis, Father Rick, and all of the activists and friends I love who have welcomed me and my family into your homes and hearts.

And to my friends who are not only the greatest actors but also the best human beings as well—Patricia Arquette, Viola Davis, Olivia Wilde, Olympia Dukakis, Chris Rock, and my joy bringer, Mariska Hargitay, you all inspire me every day with your compassion, talent, and grace.

To Susan Smalley, Yasmeen Hassan, Pat Mitchell, Jamie Wolf, Geralyn Dreyfous, Jodie Evans, Regina Scully, Gloria Steinem,

Michael Kimmel, DeVon Franklin, Anastasia Khoo, and Loreen Arbus—you are all powerful leaders fighting for equal and human rights and I am lucky to have you as guides and some of you even as friends.

To our home team—Michelle Czarnik, Gloria Aylala, Kolby Coons, Rachel de la Torre, Darcy Brislin, and Carleigh Rochon—without you our house and office would not be a home.

Thank you to Dr. Louis Fishman and Dr. Radi Shamsi, without whom I would still have millions of little parasites running around inside me!

And to my unofficial editor and great friend, Claudia Carasso, who spent many hours talking me through this process and being at my side to make sure the voice on the page matched the voice in my heart.

To all the people who helped me to grow whether it was painful or not. Some know who you are and some have no idea.

Father Ray and John Calley, you continue to give me the strength, even from Heaven, to put myself out there. I'm sure you are having a beer together right now.

To Dan McDermott, a great dad and my partner for life in raising our wonderful son.

And to the most curious, odd, beautiful, and magical Zimbabwean I've ever known, Clare Munn. I'm lucky to be walking side by side with you in this lifetime. We are mostly perfect, and without your love, this adventure would be boring.

And to Jackson—you read some things in this book that most kids would not want to know about their mothers. But you are not "most kids." I appreciate you as a human being and am so lucky to be on this journey with you. Thank you for your words "whatever, love is love." Without them, and without you, I would be lost.

x,

M

RESOURCES

Jamison, Kay Redfield. *An Unquiet Mind: A Memoir of Moods and Madness.* New York: Vintage, 1997.

Paulus, Trina. *Hope for the Flowers.* New York: Paulist Press, 1972.

Shinn, Florence Scovel. *The Game of Life and How to Play It.* Camarillo, CA: DeVorss & Company, 1978.

ABOUT THE AUTHOR

MARIA BELLO is an activist, actor, and writer. Her essay "Coming Out as a Modern Family" was one of the 10 most popular to appear in the *New York Times*'s Modern Love column. She lives in Los Angeles, California.

Maria's Whatever campaign supports human and equal rights causes. A portion of proceeds from the sale of products offered on the site will go toward supporting these organizations: HRC (hrc.org), Equality Now (equalitynow.org), and We Advance (weadvance.org).

WHATEVERLOVEISLOVE.COM